SCOUTING
REPORTS

D1315375

SCOUTING REPORTS

*The Original Reviews of Some
of Baseball's Greatest Stars*

Stan Hart

MACMILLAN • USA

All baseball cards are courtesy of
The Topps Company, Inc.

MACMILLAN
A Prentice Hall Macmillan Company
15 Columbus Circle
New York, NY 10023

Library of Congress Cataloging-in-Publication Data available
ISBN 0-02-033085-5

Manufactured in the United States of America

10 9 8 7 6 5 4 3 2 1

CONTENTS

PART II
WHAT THE SCOUTS HAVE
TO SAY ABOUT . . .

PART III

THE FOUR THAT GOT AWAY

PART IV

THE SCOUTS

INTRODUCTION

In this book we examine how some of the important ballplayers of the present and the past were evaluated by major league scouts when they were prospects in high school or college. Some of the judgments are interesting because they were right on target, and some are interesting because they weren't.

A word about scouting in general. At one time, a baseball scout had to be able to find a prospect, evaluate his potential, and sign him *before* other scouts found out about him. Scouts like Bill Essick, who first spotted Ted Williams; Paul Kritchel, who discovered Lou Gehrig; and Tom Greenwade, who saw and signed Mickey Mantle, traveled the dusty back roads of America searching for talent (as did most of the veteran scouts interviewed for this book). But today's younger scouts have never been part of the old "Find, Hide, and Sign" school of scouting. They haven't had to because of the great change that occurred in 1965.

In order to prevent dynasties from dominating baseball as the Yankees did in the thirties, fifties, and early sixties, the nondynastic clubs pushed through a rule establishing the major league draft. That meant that a team could no longer use its deep pockets to buy up all the available talent. Since 1965 each club has drafted players in the inverse order of its standing in the previous season: the first place club chooses last, the last place club first. The player drafted may be signed only by the team that drafted him. Except for the rare instance when a player is eligible but isn't drafted, he may be signed by any club as a free agent as in pre-1965 years.

The effect of the draft on scouting has been profound. Scouting became less personal, less entrepreneurial. A scout could no longer afford to spend a great deal of time cultivating a prospect as he once did. It could prove to be a waste of time, since the youngster might be taken by another team with a higher draft position.

In 1974 another element was added that further affected scouting. The Major League Scouting Bureau was formed. Its purpose was to reduce the duplication and the resulting expense of having scouts from many teams observing the same prospects. The ML Bureau hired its own scouts. However, this created an implied contradiction between the team scout and the bureau scout because they often report on the same prospect. While it's to the team scout's interest to keep the player under wraps, the Bureau scout shares his findings with all the twenty-eight major league teams. The ML Bureau had about eighty scouts until 1994, when it let thirty go. The future of the bureau seems unclear. Team scouts are divided in their opinions of the ML scouting bureau's effectiveness, as you can see in some of the interviews.

There are approximately one thousand scouts working for major league teams. Most of them are full- or part-time area scouts who follow up the prospects furnished by their information network, which consists of high school, college, American Legion, and other amateur league team coaches and umpires and, occasionally, sportswriters. Other scouts are cross-checkers, who judge the talent that the area scout has reported on. Then there are the Major League scouts who do not report on new talent. These scouts report on the strengths and weaknesses of the other Major League teams and their high minor league affiliates. This information is vital when an organization considers making trades.

A few days before the annual Major League draft, the clubs call in their scouting supervisors and cross-checkers and go over each prospect and prioritize their draft selections. Since a team will draft from fifty to seventy-five players each year, there's a lot of work to be done before the list is finalized. Originally, every team attended the draft meeting; now it's done by a telecommunications hookup.

This book is full of actual scouting reports that have been resurrected from the files of the scouts. In the cases where the actual reports were not available, we've included the reminiscences of scouts, who graciously shared their recollections with us.

In researching this book, I had the great pleasure of getting to know some of the fine men in the scouting profession. Without exception, they were all gracious, helpful, and a delight to talk to. The older scouts deserve recognition and appreciation for their enormous contributions to the game. Unfortunately, they get little of either from the baseball establishment because the front office believes that the art of baseball is the art of the deal.

I also want to give a special thanks to Tom Ferrick. He made this book possible by his kindness and special efforts on my behalf.

Thanks to an old, dear friend, Sy Berger, Executive V.P. of The Topps Company, for being so admired and respected by baseball scouts. My friendship with Sy opened many scouts' doors.

Overall future potential 66 - $50,000

Report No. 1

PLAYER MOLITOR PAUL LEO

Position SS

rent Address

ephone _____ [Area C

manent addre

am Name U.

out

R Throws

SOTA

nings 13

PART I

THE PLAYERS

RATING KEY
standing
Good
ve Average
rage
w Average
Below Average

D DESCRIPTION

600D

ty 600D

se One Grade
rade On Major
ague Standards
Not Amateur

0677

Aggressiveness		6	6	Aggressiveness				Phase
Pull	Str. Away		Opp. Field	Arm Action				REGULAR
X	X			Delivery				

Physical Description (Injuries, Glasses, etc.)   GRADUATION _____
MEDIUM BUILT- WELL PROPORTION- ON SLENDER SIDE-
IRY - LEGS ARE BOWED- STRONG BODY- NO INJURIES OR
LASSES- JUNIOR- GRADUATES 1978 -

Abilities
GGRESSIVE HITTER THAT MAKES GOOD CONTACT- HAS FAIR
WR WITH METAL BAT- GOOD QUICK STROKE - HAS GOOD HANDS
AKES DP WELL ON BOTH ENDS - ARM AVERAGE, MAY BE BETTER
VER HAVE TO MAKE QUICK THROW TO 1B - GOOD RUNR THAT CA
TEAL A BASE- GOOD BASE RUNR- KNOWS HOW TO PLAY- QUICK HANDS

Weaknesses
HITS WITH OPEN STANCE AND STEPS TOWARDS 3B A LITTLE
INSTEAD OF AT THE PITCHER- SWINGS TOO HARD, TRIES TO
HIT EVERY PITCH OUT OF PARK - I DON'T THINK HE WILL BE A
POWER HITTER-

Summation and Signability
THIS PLAYER HAS VERY GOOD ALL-AROUND ABILITY- FROM WHAT I
SAW, I DON'T THINK HE IS TOO FAR OFF FROM BEING ABLE TO
PLAY IN ML - I LIKED HIM VERY MUCH AND WOULDN'T BE AFRAI
TO HAVE HIM AS FIRST ROUND PICK-

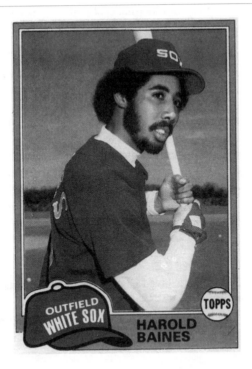

HAROLD BAINES

When master showman Bill Veeck recommended a young high school prospect to the White Sox, some in the front office must have wondered if this was another of Bill's famous put-ons.

Back in 1951, Veeck was general manager of the perennial cellar-dwelling St. Louis Browns. Attendance was miserable, so to give the numbers a boost, he hired an unknown player named Eddie Gaedel. On August 18, 1951, Gaedel went up to pinch hit for a player named Frank Saucier. The fans, who had been promised a surprise, roared with what today would be politically incorrect hilarity as Gaedel stepped to the plate. Eddie Gaedel was 3'7" tall, justifying the number on the back of his little Browns' jersey: $1/8$. After he walked, he was replaced by a pinch runner.

When Will Harridge, the president of the AL, learned of Veeck's prank, he was livid. He banned the little player and gave Veeck a tongue-lashing for daring to have some fun with our national pastime. Appalled, Harridge must have thought, Is nothing sacred?

So when Bill Veeck, who had been out of baseball for a number of years, called the White Sox to tout a player, they took his suggestion with a grain of salt. But they didn't have to, because Veeck was talking about Harold Baines, a "for real" ball player and potential major league star. Veeck became aware of Baines because Veeck's two children and Baines attended the same high school in Maryland. The White Sox looked Baines over and liked what they saw. The same can not be said of Tom Ferrick, the Royals' scout, who watched him play in a game in 1977, as the report indicates.

The White Sox, thanks to their last-place finish in 1976, had the first pick in the 1977 June draft. They chose Baines. Veeck was determined that Baines would play with the Chisox, and he personally signed the youngster, sweet-talking him into accepting a contract with a modest $40,000 bonus—the lowest bonus ever paid to a number one draft choice.

Although the Royals were wary of Baines's temperament, they never doubted his ability as a long-ball hitter. Baines hit twenty or more homers in consecutive seasons from 1982 to 1987. In three League Championship Series Baines has hit .327, and he has played in five All-Star Games.

It's interesting to note how much value is given to a prospect's attitude by a scout. It's lucky for the White Sox that Veeck saw Baines on days when he felt like playing.

KANSAS CITY ROYALS
FREE AGENT REPORT

Overall future potential __5 8__   Report No. __1__

PLAYER __BAINES__   __HAROLD__   __DOUGLAS__   Position __CF__
     Last name   First name   Middle name

Current Address __Box 35 St. Michaels__   __MD__   __MD__   __21663__
                                 City   State   Zip Code

Telephone __301- 745-4353__   Date of Birth __3/15/54__ Ht. __6 2__ Wt. __180__ Bats __L__ Throws __L__
     (Area Code)

Permanent address (if different from above) __SAME__

Team Name __ST. MICHAELS H.S.__ City __ST. MICHAELS__ State __MD__

Scout __TOM FERRICK__ Date __5/4/77__ Race __BLACK__ Games __1__ Innings __7__

RATING KEY	NON-PITCHERS	Pres.	Fut.	PITCHERS	Pres.	Fut.	USE WORD DESCRIPTION
8–Outstanding	Hitting Ability	4	6	Fast Ball			Habits _FAIR_
7–Very Good	Power	6	7	Curve			Dedication _Fair_
6–Above Average	Running Speed 4,1½	4	5	Control			Agility _Good_
5–Average	Base Running	4	5	Change of Pace			Aptitude _FAIR_
4–Below Average	Arm Strength	4	5	Slider			Phys. Maturity _Good_
3–Well Below Average	Arm Accuracy	4	5	Knuckle Ball			Emot. Maturity _Good_
2–Poor	Fielding	4	5	Other			Married _NO_
	Range	5	5	Poise			
Use One Grade	Baseball Instinct	4	5	Baseball Instinct			Date Eligible
Grade On Major	Aggressiveness	3	3	Aggressiveness			JUNE 1977
League Standards	Pull Str. Away	Opp. Field		Arm Action ___			Phase
Not Amateur	___ ✓			Delivery ___			LEG

Physical Description (Injuries, Glasses, etc.) __WIRY, STRONG. WELL BUILT ATHLETIC BODY__
__HAS HAIR DONE IN CORN ROWS, TAILS. ALSO GOATEE.__

Abilities __GOOD BAT SPEED. SHORT QUICK STROKE. HANDS O.K. RANGE__
__FAIR HAS + POWER__

Weaknesses __DOES NOT ACT VERY CONCERNED OR INTERESTED IN PLAYING.__
__WILL LUNGE AT BREAKING STUFF__

Summation and Signability __HAS GOOD BAT POTENTIAL. DEFENSE AS 1B , ARM__
__M.L. AVERAGE. ARM SHORT FROM OF. DEFENSE IN OF ADEQUATE__
__ONLY MY OPINION BUT THIS PLAYER COULD BE MORE TROUBLE__
__THAN HE IS WORTH. TOOK 5 POINTS OFF FOR GENERAL ATTITUDE.__

SCOTT BANKHEAD

*T*he Kansas City Royals were right about Scott Bankhead, twice. The first time was when he was scouted as a pitcher for the University of North Carolina. In his senior year he compiled a brilliant 11–0 record with a microscopic 1.60 ERA, and he was elected to the 1984 U.S. Olympic Baseball Team. The Royals selected Bankhead as their first draft choice in 1984. He had previously been drafted as a senior at Reidsville High in the Tar Heel State by the Pirates, but he had chosen to go to college instead.

Bankhead spent less than two years in the minors before being called up to Kansas City in 1986, where he had an 8–9 record. In December of that year, the Royals were right about Bankhead for the second time. They traded him to Seattle with two other players to get Danny Tartabull. Tartabull became one of the AL's top home-run hitters while Bankhead has had the misfortune of going on the DL for extended periods of time.

In 1987 Bankhead won 9 games for the Mariners and spent almost a month on the DL. But the worst was yet to come. The following year Bankhead was out of action almost the entire season, and in 1991 he again spent most of his time on the DL trying to get healthy. In 1992, as a free agent, he signed a one-year contract with Cincinnati, where he enjoyed his most productive season. Used exclusively as a relief pitcher, Bankhead posted a 10–4 record with a 2.93 ERA.

Bankhead was a free agent again at the end of the season, so he decided to try his luck back in the AL. Maybe he shouldn't have. Signing with Boston, Bankhead saw limited action in 1993, pitching in 64 1/3 innings with a 3.50 ERA and two wins in three decisions. In 1994 he was once again on the DL early in May.

KANSAS CITY ROYALS
FREE AGENT REPORT

OFFICE USE
Report No. _____
Player No. _____

Overall Future Potential _____ 65

Nat'l. Double Check   Yes __✓__ No_____

Scout's Report # _____ 1

Scout_____ FERRICK

Date___ 4/21/84

PLAYER ___ BANKHEAD MICHAEL SCOTT ___ TEAM NAME ___ U. oF N.C. ___ Pos. _ RHP
Last Name   First Name   Middle Initial

Permanent Address ___ 1003 RIDGEWOOD AVE REIDSVILLE NC 27320   919-767-5144
Street   City   St   Zip   Phone

Current Address ___ F10 CAROLINA APTS CARRBORO N.C. 27570   919-967-8524
Street   City   St   Zip   Phone

Date of Birth _07/31/63_ Ht. _5.10_ Wt. _175_ Bats _R_ Throws _R_ PHASE _R_ DATE ELIGIBLE _6/84_

Game Date(s) ___ APR 19 '84 Games ___ 1 ___ Innings ___ 7 ___ Graduation ___ 6/85

No.	RATING KEY	M.P.H.	NON-PITCHERS	Pres.	Fut.	PITCHERS	Pres.	Fut.	MAKEUP				
8	Outstanding	94-	Hitting Ability			Fast Ball	5	5					
7	Very Good	91-93	Power			Life of Fastball	4	5		Ex.	Good	Fair	Poor
6	Above Average	88-90	Running Speed			Curve	4	5	Habits	4	3	2	1
5	Average	85-87	Base Running			Control	5	6	Dedication	4	3	2	1
4	Below Average	82-84	Arm Strength			Change of pace	4	5	Agility	4	3	2	1
3	Well Below Ave.	79-81	Arm Accuracy			Slider	4	5	Aptitude	4	3	2	1
2	Poor	0-78	Fielding			Other	—	—	Phys. Mat.	4	3	2	1
			Range			Poise	6	6	Emot. Mat.	4	3	2	1

USE ONE GRADE	Hitting: (√)	Running		EX	GOOD	FAIR	POOR		Baseball Inst.	4	3	2	1
Grade On	Pull ....3 _____	Time To	Arm Action	4	3	2	1		Aggressive-	4	3	2	1
Major League	St. Away ....2 _____	1st Base		3/4	OH	SIDE	OTHER		ness				
Standard	Opp. Field.. 1 _____		Delivery	4	3	2	1		OVERALL	4	3	2	1
			Gun Reading _86_ to _88_ MPH										

Physical Description (Injuries, Glasses, etc.) MEDIUM HEIGHT - STURDY FRAME . SERIOUS +
ARDENT CONDITIONER. HAD DELTOID (SHOULDER) STRAIN EARLIER.
OK NOW. NO GLASSES.

Abilities   AVERAGE ML. F.B. TALKS AT TIMES . SLIDER CAN BE AVER.
AT TIMES. SLIGHT DOWNWARD TAIL. CURVE GOOD SPIN + ROTAT-
-ION THOUGH DOES NOT HAVE QUICK BITE. COMMAND — POISE GOOD
STICH NOT TOO BAD.

Weaknesses   SLOW RELEASE WITH MEN ON BASE.

Signability: Ex. _____ Good __✓__ Fair _____ Poor _____ Worth: $ _____

Makeup Evaluation and Player Summation   SHOULD GO IN ML. DRAFT. HAS THE EQUIPMENT — DESIRE
+ COMPETITIVE MAKE UP. SHOULD TAKE BUT 2YRS TO GET TO M.L.
PERHAPS LESS. I LIKE HIS CHANCES.

JAY BELL

*J*ay is one of the few Pirates left from the fine Pittsburgh teams of
'90, '91, and '92. Bonds, Bonilla, and Drabek have all gone on to
fame and fortune elsewhere, and the fortunes of the Pirates seemed to
have gone with them. From winning the NL East pennant in 1992 by nine
games, the Pirates toppled to fifth place, twenty-two games out in 1993
despite the fact that Jay Bell had his best year, batting a career high .310 in
154 games.

Drafted after high school by the Minnesota Twins in the first round
of the 1984 draft, Jay was traded the next year to Cleveland and spent two
more seasons in the minors before being called up at the end of 1986.
Jay's debut was awe-inspiring. In his first at bat, on the first pitch, against
Minnesota, he participated in setting a record—Bert Blyleven's. Jay's blast
was the forty-seventh of the season given up by Blyleven, who went on

9

to give up three more for an unenviable record-setting 50 home runs allowed by a pitcher in one season. In 1989 Jay was traded to Pittsburgh.

Very sure-handed in the field, Jay led the NL in putouts and assists in both '92 and '93. His remarkable .986 fielding average in '93 was also tops for the NL and he committed only eleven errors in 154 games and was voted to the NL All-Star team.

Jay's three partial seasons with the Indians were as painful as his .223 BA attests. But in the NL, Jay has batted fifty points higher. In the 1991 NL East Championship Series, Jay led the Pirates with a .414 BA with 12 hits in the seven games. Although he has been in three division championship series, Jay has yet to play in a World Series game. Since the Pirates seem to be on a "divest and self-destroy" mission by letting most of their best players find other venues, perhaps Jay will get a chance for a World Series ring with another team in the future.

MAJOR LEAGUE SCOUTING BUREAU
FREE AGENT REPORT

Overall future potential __60.7__   Report No. __1__

PLAYER __Bell__ (Last name) __JAY__ (First name) __STUART__ (Middle name)   Position __SS__

Current Address __9752 QUAIL HOLLOW CT.__ __PENSACOLA__ (City) __FLA__ (State) __32514__ (Zip Code)

Telephone __904-477-0290__ (Area Code)   Date of Birth __11-04-64__ Ht. __6'1"__ Wt. __175__ Bats __R__ Throws __R__

Permanent address (If different from above) __SAME__

Team Name __TATe H.S.__   City __GONZALEZ__   State __FLA__

Scout __D. BOGARD__   Date __03-17-84__   Games __2__   Innings __10__

RATING KEY	NON-PITCHERS		Pres.	Fut.	PITCHERS		Pres.	Fut.	USE WORD DESCRIPTION
8–Outstanding	Hitting Ability	✓ *	4	6	Fast Ball	*			Habits __good__
7–Very Good	Power	✓ *	5	6	Curve	*			Dedication __good__
6–Above Average	Running Speed	*	5	5	Control				Agility __good__
5–Average	Base Running		5	5	Change of Pace				Aptitude __good__
4–Below Average	Arm Strength	✓ *	5	6	Slider	*			Phys. Maturity __good__
3–Well Below Average	Arm Accuracy		5	6	Knuckle Ball				Emot. Maturity __good__
2–Poor	Fielding	*	4	5	Other	*			Married
	Range		4	4	Poise				
USE ONE GRADE	Baseball Instinct		5	6	Baseball Instinct				Date Eligible
Grade On Major	Aggressiveness		6	6	Aggressiveness				
League Standards	Pull		Str. Away		Opp. Field		Arm Action		Phase
Not Amateur	X						Delivery		Reg.

Physical Description (Injuries, Glasses, etc.)   GRADUATION __06-84__

AVe. HT. Well PReP. ATHLETIC BUILD. MUSCULAR LEGS.

Abilities

AGG. WITH BAT SHORT STROKE, good BAT SPeed. WAITS ON BALL Well. HARD CONTACT WITH BALL. FAIR ACTIONS IN FIELD. SURe HANDS, STRONG ARM. AVe RUNNeR, HUSTLeR, PLAYS HARD.

Weaknesses

FIeLDS BALL TOO CLOSe TO BODY. DOe'S NOT USe FeeT WeLL WHeN THROWING.

Summation and Signability   Worth ~~Majors~~

ABOVe AVe. POT. WITH BAT. CAN MAKe ROUTINe PLAYS AT SS, BUT LACKS THe QUICKNESS OF MIDDIE INF. TOOLS MAY Be BeST SUITED FOR 3B OR OF.

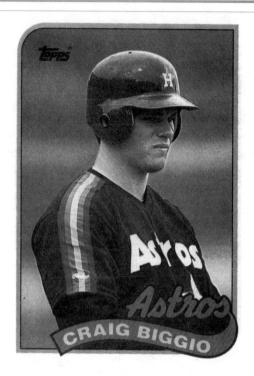

CRAIG BIGGIO

*I*f you're a scout and you have your stopwatch out and the kid catcher you're timing gets down to first in 4.1 seconds, you should do one of two things: either check your watch or get down on your knees and pray that no other scout has seen him. That's how fast Craig Biggio was and still is. When he was a junior at Seton Hall University in New Jersey, he was part of a sensational team. Playing along with Biggio was freshman Mo Vaughn, who now hits monster homers for the Boston Red Sox. As can be imagined, the team attracted a lot of attention.

Biggio didn't hit with as much power as Vaughn, but his overall numbers at Seton Hall were very impressive. He hit .407 with 14 homers in his last year, and the Royals were high on him. But Kansas City needed a good young pitcher and opted for Kevin Appier as their first-round choice in the 1987 draft. By the time the Royals got to the second round, Biggio was gone, grabbed by Houston.

Biggio started his pro career like a house on fire. When the college season ended, the Astros sent him to Asheville in the South Atlantic League, where he hit .375 in 64 games. He also stole 31 bases and raised a lot of eyebrows. A catcher who steals bases? At Asheville Biggio also started playing the outfield. He was brought up by Houston during the 1988 season after spending only a year and a half in minor league ball. In 1993 Biggio led the Astros in runs scored, as he had done the previous year, and he also demonstrated new-found power by hitting 41 doubles and 26 homers to lead the team in those departments as well.

Although Biggio quickly became one of the best defensive catchers in the NL, he was switched to second base full time in 1992. At that position he also became one of the league's finest defensive players, leading NL in putouts and, in 1993, leading in assists. Biggio's speed continues to make opposing pitchers and catchers crazy. In 1992 he led the Astros with 38 stolen bases.

Like a dedicated fisherman, Tom Ferrick—who scouted Biggio for the Royals—can't forget the big one that got away.

KANSAS CITY ROYALS
FREE AGENT REPORT

OFFICE USE
Report No. _____
Player No. _____

Overall Future Potential _____ 60

Nat'l. Double Check Yes __✓__ No_____

Scout's Report # _____ 1

Scout ____ FERRICK

PLAYER ___ BIGGIO _____ CRAIG _____ Pos. ___ C ___ Date ___ APR 15 87
    Last Name   First Name   Middle Initial

School or Team ___ SETON HALL UNIVERSITY City and State ___ S. ORANGE ___ NJ

Permanent Address _____ Street _____ City _____ St _____ Zip _____ Phone

Current Address _____ Street _____ City _____ St _____ Zip _____ Phone

Date of Birth _____ Ht. _6.0_ Wt. _185_ Bats _R_ Throws _R_ DATE ELIGIBLE _JUNE 87_ PHASE _R_

Game Date(s) __ APR 15 1987 Games ___ 3 ___ Innings ___ 21 ___ Graduation ___ JUNE '88

No.	RATING KEY	M.P.H.	NON-PITCHERS	Pres.	Fut.	PITCHERS	Pres.	Fut.	MAKEUP				
8	Outstanding	94-	Hitting Ability	3	4	Fast Ball							
7	Very Good	91-93	Power	3	3	Life of Fastball				Ex.	Good	Fair	Poor
6	Above Average	88-90	Running Speed	7	7	Curve			Habits	4	✓	2	1
5	Average	85-87	Base Running	5	5	Control			Dedication	4	✓	2	1
4	Below Average	82-84	Arm Strength	5	5	Change of Pace			Agility	✓	3	2	1
3	Well Below Ave.	79-81	Arm Accuracy	5	6	Slider			Aptitude	4	✓	2	1
2	Poor	0-78	Fielding	5	6	Other			Phys. Mat.	4	✓	2	1
			Range	5	6	Poise			Emot. Mat.	4	✓	2	1

USE ONE GRADE	Hitting: (√)	Running						Baseball Inst.	4	✓	2	1
Grade On	Pull .... 3 ✓	Time To		EX	GOOD	FAIR	POOR	Aggressive-	4	✓	2	1
Major League	St. Away .... 2 ____	1st Base		4	3	2	1	ness				
Standard	Opp. Field .. 1 ____	4.0 4.1	Arm Action	3/4	OH	SIDE	OTHER	OVERALL	4	✓	2	1
			Delivery	4	3	2	1					
		Gun Reading ____ to ____ MPH										

Physical Description (Injuries, Glasses, etc.) WIRM - LIVE BODY. NO GLASSES. NO KNOWN INJURIES. WELL PROPORTIONED

Abilities AGGRESSIVE - TAKE CHARGE TYPE. NOT AFRAID OF CONTACT AT PLATE. QUICK - AGILE IN ALL MOVEMENTS. HANDS - RECEIVING - BLOCKS BALL IN DIRT WELL. ARM - SML - CLOSE TO 6 ML. QUICK RELEASE. ALERT → IN GAME - HUSTLES WELL - FAIR CONTACT WITH BAT. LINE DRIVE TYPE HITTER

Weaknesses NONE APPARENT AT THIS TIME.

Signability: Ex. _____ Good _____ Fair ✓ Poor _____ Worth: $ 55-60000
    MIKE SHEPARD - COACH - ALWAYS GETS INVOLVED IN SOME WAY WITH SIGNING HIS PLAYERS. CAN BE TOUGH.

Makeup Evaluation and Player Summation GOOD MAKEUP- MENTALLY TOUGH. HAS THE PHYSICAL TOOLS TO BE M.L. CATCHER. NOT A POWER HITTER. CONTACT + LINE DRIVE TYPE. HIS BAT WILL DETERMINE NO.1 OR 2 STATUS. CAN ALSO STEAL BASES. GOOD SPEED FOR CATCHER.

VIDA BLUE

*I*n the mid-sixties, the Kansas City A's (as they were known before their move to Oakland the following year) learned of a schoolboy phenom and dispatched scout Tom Ferrick to check him out. Tom flew down to New Orleans and went up to Mansfield, Louisiana, to a game between two black high schools. "My assistant and I were the only white people among the 4,000 black high school kids. We really stood out. Everyone must have known why we were there." That day, Blue showed his remarkable stuff, and Ferrick reported his findings back to the club.

In the 1967 draft, Kansas City picked Vida Blue and held their breath. Blue was also a quarterback with a deadly accurate arm. The University of Houston wanted him, and so did Grambling. As his scouting report shows, the A's felt they could get him for $15–20,000 plus college expenses. But suddenly, Blue's father died.

Now the breadwinner of a large family, Blue knew that $15–20,000 wouldn't last very long. He needed more money. If the A's wouldn't meet his number, then Blue could threaten to start college. In that case, the A's pick would be nullified, Blue would be placed back into the draft when he became eligible after his junior year, and the A's would have to wait their turn. By that time, if the A's scouts were right, other teams would be lined up to grab him as their first choice.

Was Blue bluffing? We'll never really know because, after a lot of "you push—I'll pull" negotiations, the A's parted with $40,000 and Blue was theirs.

His first season in the minors, 1968, was a learning experience for Blue, who posted an 8–11 record in Class A ball. But it was also a learning experience for the batters he faced. He struck out 231 of them, which factors out to over thirteen Ks per nine innings. In 1970, with the Iowa Oaks of the American Association, Vida had a 12–3 record in only seventeen games. He was called up to the parent Oakland A's at the end of the season. But the season didn't end there for Blue. On September 21, two months after his 21st birthday, Blue pitched a no-hitter against Minnesota. He was someone AL batters could look forward to in the coming seasons—with dread.

The following year, 1971, Blue had an eye-popping 24–8 record, a 1.82 ERA, and an average of one strikeout in each of the 312 innings he pitched. Blue won the Cy Young Award and was voted the AL MVP, the youngest player ever to be so honored.

Blue helped start the Oakland dynasty that had a lock on first place in the West from 1971 through 1975. When he was traded to San Francisco in 1978, the Giants had to part with seven players and $390,000 to get him. It was the biggest deal of the decade.

"Vida should have made it into the Hall of Fame, but he got derailed," said Ferrick. "He ran with party people instead of tending to business and never had the years he should have had." Blue's drug bust and his six-month suspension in 1983 marked the untimely end to what should have been one of the great pitching careers in baseball.

TOM FERRICK

MAY 16 1967 _Date_ _____

PROSPECT FOLLOW-UP REPORT
(Please print or type)

BLUE VIDA _____ Pos. _L.H.P._
(Last Name) (First Name) (Middle Init.)

Seen in Action _____ MAY 16 1967
(Month) (Day) (Year)

With _DESOTO H.S. (MANSFIELD CA.)_ Club
BETHUNE H.S. (SHREVESPORT LA.) Club
MANSFIELD _LA._
(City) (State)

REGULAR SEASON Tournament

Check:

☑ Suggest he be signed immediately or when eligible to sign.
☐ Suggest we look at him again.
☐ Suggest his file be closed.

Recommended for signing, fill in the following:

Definite ML prospect ✓ Date Eligible to Sign _JUNE 1967_
Fringe ML Prospect   Number games seen
Start in class _ROOKIE_ to date _____ / _____
Stop Watch Time to First Base _____

SCORING KEY Grade on Major League Standards— not Amateur.		Present	Future	PITCHERS	Present	Future
	Hitting Ability			Fast Ball	3	2
	Power			Curve	4	3
Outstanding	Base running			Control	4	3
	Arm (strength)			Change of Pace	NONE	
Above ML Av.	Arm (accuracy)			Slider	NONE	
	Field			Other Pitches	NONE	
	Range			Field	4	3
Average	Baseball Instinct			Baseball Instinct	4	3
Below ML Av.	Straight Pull ___ Away ___	Opposite Field ___				
	Habits			Habits	GOOD	
Poor	Aggressive ___			Aggressive	FAIR	

Physical Description: 6:00 - 190 · STURDY ATH-LETIC PHYSIQUE. GOOD LEGS. LONG ARMS + BIG HANDS. FOOTBALL PLAYER (BACK FIELD) NOT MUSCLE BOUND. LONG LOOSE 3/4 DELIVERY. FLEXIBLE LIVE ARM.

Abilities SHOWED QUITE A FEW 2 FBS ("OUTSTANDING" RATING) & 3 FBS ("ABOVE ML AVG." RATING) GOOD BODY CONTROL. RHYTHM GOOD. CAN SHOW YOU OVER POWERING FB 50% OF THE TIME. FLEXIBLE ARM. CAN (THROW) 3/4, OVERHAND & SIDEARM NATURALLY. SHOWS SOME CURVE POTENTIAL. GOOD MOVE TO 2B, (ODDLY ENOUGH) BETTER TO 1B. FINE PICK.

Weaknesses: OVER SLIDES IN DELIVERING BALL. REAL LONG STRIDE. LANDS ON LEFT HEEL. CURVE FLAT. NEEDS HELP IN MOST PHASES OF PITCHING STARTING WITH DELIVERY FIRST. SLOW MOVING BUT CAN RUN.

Summation and other comments including any information that may have bearing on his signing or not signing at this time.

HAS MAJOR LEAGUE ARM & BODY. SHOW 2 VELOCITY QUITE OFTEN DESPITE BAD DELIVERY. MAJOR LEAGUE PROSPECT. C STUDENT FATHER DEAD. OLDEST OF 6 CHILDREN WILL TAKE COLLEGE PLUS $15,000 OR $20,000. GRAMBLING COLLEGE INTERESTED IN BOY.

What should we offer:

Follow copy to Director of Scouting. Keep white copy for your file.

1976 RECORD BREAKER
GEORGE BRETT • ROYALS

**MOST CONSECUTIVE GAMES,
3-OR-MORE HITS**

ROY BRANCH /
GEORGE BRETT

*F*inding a quality prospect who the scout feels has major league potential is one thing; obtaining the rights to sign him is quite another—which takes us to the positively labyrinthine process known as the Major League draft. It is a harrowing, nail-biting journey for the scouts as well as the front office. What is required for success at baseball's version of "Dungeons and Dragons" is good judgement, which is granted to mortals, and the power of prognostication, which is not—plus a hell of a lot of luck.

Case in point: George Brett.

Any reader who doesn't know who George Brett is should be ashamed. In four years, when he becomes eligible, Brett will be inducted into the Hall of Fame. Enough said. But let's go back to 1971, when he was in El Segundo High School in California. Like his three brothers, Brett was born to play the game. His older brother Ken was getting his career in gear as a pitcher for the Red Sox, and he would go on to play thirteen years in the majors.

In 1971 Southern California was rich with baseball prospects. Reports of young phenoms rivaled UFO sightings. But George Brett's talent was for real, and when scout Rosey Gilhousen saw him play shortstop for his El Segundo school, visions of sugarplums danced in Rosey's head. To check on the recommendations of Kansas City's area scouts in the impending 1971 June draft, the Royals front office dispatched scout Tom Ferrick to the West Coast. There, he checked on, among other prospects, George Brett. Ferrick saw Brett play on April 30 and again on June 2, and he promptly filed a report.

Brett had led his high school team to the California championship and looked good. Not great, good. His range at shortstop was limited and Tom sensed that he had a "hippy problem," a reference to the distribution of Brett's 205 pounds over a 6-foot frame. It's not unusual for shortstops to go six feet or better; what is unusual is for them to weigh more than 170 pounds. Brett's size limited his ability to go wide to his left even though he was fast on the basepaths. But his bat was impressive. Tom Ferrick agreed with Gilhousen's appraisal and recommended Brett to Kansas City as a high draft choice. However, the Royals had someone else in mind for number one.

That year there was a schoolboy pitcher in St. Louis who was a "can't-miss" if there ever was one. You could bet the farm on this kid and rest easy. He had fashioned himself after the great Cardinal pitcher Bob Gibson and had a fastball that was a missile—sailing over the plate at more than ninety miles per hour. In addition, he had a beautifully vicious curve ball that sent baffled batters back to their benches—if not to their chiropractors. His name is Roy Branch, and his story goes like this.

The Royals, who drafted fifth, decided to go for Branch as their number one pick. That choice would surely mean giving up George Brett, because he would likely be chosen by one of the first four picks.

While the Royals were devising their strategy, word came from St. Louis that Roy Branch had hurt his arm in a tryout with the Cardinals and had walked off the field in pain. What to do? Should they switch their strategy and go for Brett or stay with Branch and hope that the kid, who wouldn't be eighteen for another month, could shake it off? Everyone was thinking about dipping curves and 90+ m.p.h. fastballs. They stayed with Branch. And prayed.

Roy Branch was selected by the Royals as planned, and the other teams didn't seem to know that George Brett existed. As the first round crept to its painfully slow conclusion, Brett was not selected by any team. Time for another prayer. The second round began and again Brett was the Claude Rains of the 1971 draft. When the Royals got another chance—after the White Sox, Padres, Braves, and Expos had passed Brett by a second time—they grabbed him.

19

The Royals signed both Branch and Brett and sent them down for seasoning. Branch's arm problems did not go away—they got worse. He underwent elbow surgery and sat out the next season in rehab. From there, Branch's story gets sadder. He couldn't regain his schoolboy brilliance and was never brought up by the Royals. His only Major League experience was two unsuccessful starts for Seattle in 1979. (He was never issued a Major League baseball card.) After that his life started to unravel. He was busted for drug possession while playing in Mexico in 1982 and spent eight months in a Mexican jail. In 1990, his baseball career over, he started to rebuild his life.

George Brett became one of the game's great players the hard way. He had to learn to play third and first base, where range is less of a problem, and he matured in the crucible of major league competition. When he was in the minors, his three-year BA was .281. Brett's batting average for his twenty-one major league seasons is twenty-four points higher at .305, including .340 lifetime in six championship series and .373 in two World Series. He was MVP in 1980. Brett had over three thousand hits during his career, a milestone reached by only sixteen other players in the history of the game.

As for the power of prayer, the Royals were one for two in 1971—but what a one that was.

KANSAS CITY ROYALS FREE AGENT PROSPECT REPORT

Type Prospect (check one)
Excellent ___✓___ uPPeR
Good _____
Regular Phase ✓ Secondary Phase ___
Subject for Selection _JUNE_ , 19 _71_

Month __APR__
Day __30__
Year __1971__

PLAYER INFORMATION (PRINT OR TYPE)   SCOUT __Tom FERRICK__

Name __BRETT__ (LAST) __GEORGE__ (FIRST) (MIDDLE)
Pos __SS__ Height __6:1__ Weight __193__ Bats __L__ Throws __R__
Address _____ Phone _____
City/State/Zip _____
School (HS/College) __EL SEGUNDO H.S.__ City/State/Zip __EL SEGUNDO, CAL__
Date of Birth _____ Date of Graduation (HS/College) _____
Parent's Name _____ Phone _____
Address _____ City/State/Zip _____
Family Physician _____ Phone _____
Military Status _____ Draft Priority # _____ Legion Player Yes ☐ No ☐
Has player ever been selected in F.A. Draft? Yes ☐ No ☐ If yes, by what club (s) and when? _____

Does this player have any health problems? _____
Married Yes ☐ No ☑ Glasses Yes ☐ No ☑ Physical Build __Good__
Is this player generally known by other clubs? _____ Can player be signed? _____
Bonus expected _____ Bonus recommended _____
How badly does this player want to play professional baseball? _____
How many times have you been in player's house this year? _____ last year? _____

PLAYER JUDGEMENT 1 (EXCELLENT) 2 (GOOD) 3 (FAIR) 4 (POOR) (Use +'s only)

Observtion Period–Years _____ Games __2__ Workouts _____

Non-Pitchers
Running Speed (actual) __4.4__ Base Running Ability __3__ Aggressiveness on Bases __3__
Arm Strength __+3__ Arm Accuracy __3__ Fielding __3__ Hands ____ Range __+3__
Hitting __3__ Power __3__ Frequency of Power __3__

Pitchers
Fast Ball ____ Liveliness ____ Curve ____ Change ____ Other ____
Control ____ Delivery OH ☐ 3/4 ☐ S.A. ☐ Loose Arm ____
Fielding ____ Poise ____ Other ____

All Players
Desire __3__ Baseball Intelligence __3__ Habits __3__
Competitor __3__ Aggressiveness __3__ Body Control __3__

Do you have good knowledge on this player's makeup? _____
Player should start in: ☐ RL ☐ D ☐ C ☐ Other _____

KC 6A
Original to office   **USE REVERSE SIDE FOR COMMENTS**

SAW AT SAWTELLE IN TWI-NIGHT GAME VS. MURPHY HS.
SHOWED GOOD +3 ARM AND MADE PLAY FROM HOLE.
M.L. PLAY, RANGE + HANDS. BODY CONTROL GOOD. SHOWED
SOME "POP" IN HIS BAT. PULLED BALL SHARPLY TO RF.
RUNS 4.2.

LATE BLOOMING. ROSEY WILL WATCH FOR REST
OF YEAR. COULD GO HIGH IF HE CONTINUES TO
DEVELOP. I LIKE HIS ACTIONS ON THE FIELD -
MAY HAVE "HIPPY" PROBLEM.

RIGHT NOW CHANCE BUT COULD MOVE UP.
BROTHER KENNETH BRETT LHP. RED SOX.

JUNE 2, 1971
SAW IN C.I.F. CHAMPIONSHIP GAME
VS. LOMPOC @ ANAHEIM STADIUM. PERFORMED WELL.
I WOULD UPGRADE HANDS TO +3. RANGE TO LEFT
NOT TOO GOOD. FEEL HE WOULD PLAY JUST ADEQUATE
S.S. HAS +3 ARM. AGGRESSIVE. GOOD ACTIONS. BAT
POTENTIAL WITH SOME POWER. RUNS 4.2. FEEL HE
WILL DEFINITELY GO IN M.L DRAFT - IN FIRST
TEN.

KANSAS CITY ROYALS FREE AGENT PROSPECT REPORT

Type Prospect (check one)
Excellent _____
Good ___✓___
Regular Phase __✓__ Secondary Phase____
Subject for Selection ___JUNE___, 19 _71_

Month _____MAY_____
Day _____14_____
Year _____1971_____

PLAYER INFORMATION (PRINT OR TYPE)   SCOUT ___TOM FERRICK___

Name ___BRANCH (LAST)___ ___ROY (FIRST)___ ___(MIDDLE)___

Pos _L HP._ Height _5 11_ Weight _185_ Bats _R_ Throws _R_

Address _____ Phone _____

City/State/Zip _____

School (HS/College) _BEAUMONT H.S._ City/State/Zip _ST LOUIS, MO._

Date of Birth _____ Date of Graduation (HS/College) _____

Parent's Name _____ Phone _____

Address _____ City/State/Zip _____

Family Physician _____ Phone _____

Military Status _____ Draft Priority # _____ Legion Player Yes ☐ No ☐

Has player ever been selected in F.A. Draft? Yes ☐ No ☐ If yes, by what club (s) and when? _____

Does this player have any health problems? _____

Married Yes ☐ No ☐   Glasses Yes ☐ No ☑   Physical Build _GOOD_

Is this player generally known by other clubs? _____ Can player be signed? _____

Bonus expected _____ Bonus recommended _____

How badly does this player want to play professional baseball? _____

How many times have you been in player's house this year? _____ last year? _____

PLAYER JUDGEMENT 1 (EXCELLENT) 2 (GOOD) 3 (FAIR) 4 (POOR) (Use +'s only)

Observtion Period–Years _____ Games ___1___ Workouts _____

Non-Pitchers

Running Speed (actual) _____ Base Running Ability _____ Aggressiveness on Bases _____

Arm Strength _____ Arm Accuracy _____ Fielding _____ Hands _____ Range _____

Hitting _____ Power _____ Frequency of Power _____

Pitchers

Fast Ball _+3+3_ Liveliness _+3_ Curve _+3.3_ Change _____ Other _SLIDER 3_

Control _3_ Delivery OH ☐ 3/4 ☑ S.A. ☐ Loose Arm _GOOD_

Fielding _3_ Poise _+3_ Other _____

All Players

Desire _____ Baseball Intelligence _3_ Habits _____

Competitor _+3_ Aggressiveness _3_ Body Control _+3_

Do you have good knowledge on this player's makeup? _____

Player should start in: ☐ RL ☐ D ☐ C ☐ Other _____

KC 6A
Original to office

USE REVERSE SIDE FOR COMMENTS

23

Saw in day game @ St. Louis
Showed good poise + also good competitive
qualities in 7 inn. game. Pitching with only two
days rest: Long arms - big hands. Has some
growing room. Body control + coordination good.

Live arm. Showed +3.3 vel. on FB. Also
good rotation on curve +3.3.

    Appeared tired in 4th inn. But kept
firing. Struck out last two hitters with
men on 2nd + 3rd base after some errors.

    Would like to have seen him with
more than 2 days rest. But still impressive.

    Good M.L. prospect.
Could go in top five in M.L. draft.

KEVIN BROWN

*I*n 1986 Brown was chosen by the *Sporting News* for their college All-America team on the strength of an 11–5 record and 3.57 ERA in his last season at Georgia Tech. In that year's draft he was signed by the Rangers as their first choice. Although he played in six games in the minors in '86, it wasn't until the end of the season that he got his first victory in organized baseball, and that was with the parent Rangers in the American League. Sent down the following season to gain more experience, Brown didn't overwhelm the opposition when he pitched for Tulsa, Oklahoma City, and Charlotte. But in 1988, when he was back at Tulsa, Brown posted an impressive 12–10 record and was recalled late in the season by Texas, where he posted a 1–1 mark with a 4.24 ERA.

In 1989 at Texas he won 12 games, lost 9, and had a 3.35 ERA with seven complete games, a high for the team. In the next two years his control was trouble-some, and his strikeouts-to-bases-on-balls ratio dropped. However, Brown still managed to win twelve games in 1990 and had seven complete games, a high for the Rangers. He slipped to a 9–12 mark in 1991 and had the dubious distinc-tion of hitting thirteen batters. Brown regained his form and was sensational in 1992. His SO/BB ratio improved dramatically and his twenty-one victories tied him with Jack Morris for Most AL wins. Brown was the starting pitcher in the '92 All-Star game, in which he pitched one inning of hitless, shutout ball in the AL's trouncing of the National League. Brown finished the season with eleven complete games and placed seventh in strikeouts with 173.

He continued to be one of the AL's premiere strikeout kings in 1993, with 142 Ks, a 15–12 record and a 3.59 ERA. His twelve complete games that year was second to Angel Chuck Finley's league-leading thirteen.

TEXAS RANGERS
FREE AGENT REPORT

Overall future potential __65__   Report No. __1__

PLAYER __Brown__ (Last name) __James__ (First name) __Kevin__ (Middle name)   Position __RHP__

Current Address __P.O. Box 33327__ __Atlanta__ (City) __Ga__ (State) __30332__ (Zip Code)

Telephone __(404)__ (Area Code) __676-0921__   Date of Birth __03/14/65__ Ht. __6'4__ Wt. __195__ Bats __R__ Throws __L__

Permanent address (if different from above) __Rt. 1 McIntyre, Ga. 31054.__

Team Name __Georgia Tech__   City __Atlanta__   State __Ga__

Scout __Hancock__   Date __4-19-86__ Race ____ Games __3__ Innings __18 2/3 inn.__

RATING KEY	NON-PITCHERS	Pres.	Fut.	PITCHERS	Pres.	Fut.	USE WORD DESCRIPTION
8—Outstanding	Hitting Ability	*		Fast Ball	* 6	7	Habits _Good_
7—Very Good	Power	*		Curve	*		Dedication _Good_
6—Above Average	Running Speed	*		Control	5	6	Agility _Good_
5—Average	Base Running			Change of Pace	3	5	Aptitude _Good_
4—Below Average	Arm Strength	*		Slider	* 5	6	Phys. Maturity _Excel_
3—Well Below Average	Arm Accuracy			Knuckle Ball			Emot. Maturity _Good_
2—Poor	Fielding	*		Other	*		Married _No_
	Range			Poise	5	5	
Use One Grade	Baseball Instinct			Baseball Instinct	5	5	Date Eligible _6-86_
Grade On Major	Aggressiveness			Aggressiveness	7	7	
League Standards	Pull Str. Away Opp. Field			Arm Action _Good_ A 3/4			Phase
Not Amateur	___ ___			Delivery _Good_			_Reg_

Physical Description (Injuries, Glasses, etc.)   GRADUATION __6-87__

Home Phone
(912) 946-2228

Tall, thin, strong body. Broad shoulders. Long arms.

Tendonitis - rt. elbow
Hurt orig. Hawaii

Abilities Above avg. FB with plus movement. Boring, sinking action. Slider has good bite occasionally. Free and easy arm action. A competitor. A little mean if he has to be.

Weaknesses Slider is not consistent. Slows arm and motion on change.

Best arm I've seen. Does not have know-how that Swindell has.

Summation and Signability   Worth _____

Great competitor with great arm. Has come a long way and probably not finished yet. Should be a solid #1 type starter. Hope we get him nL next yr.

FB-86-93   SL 79-83

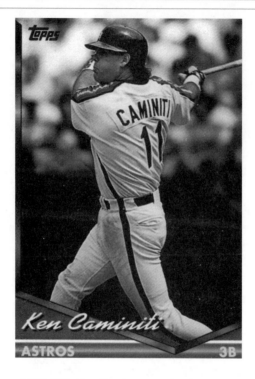

KEN CAMINITI

*A*fter having been selected as the third baseman on the *Sporting News* All-America college team in 1984, Caminiti was picked by the Astros in the third round of that year's draft. He broke in with Osceola of the Florida State League in '85, and his .284 BA earned him a promotion to Columbus of the Southern Association for the '86 season. There, Caminiti batted .300 with 12 homers and 81 RBI's. In '87, after hitting .325 in 95 games for Columbus, he was brought up to Houston for the rest of the season. After one more year in the minors at Tucson, he came to the majors to stay.

In 1991 Caminiti convincingly demonstrated his run-producing talent by driving in 80 runs with 13 Astro homers, tying for second with Luis Gonzalez, behind Jeff Bagwell's 15. The following season, '92, he had the best Houston batting average with .294 and again was second in homers with 13. He hit 13 homers for the third straight season in 1993 and drove in 75 runs.

In 1994 Caminiti started fast and demonstrated new-found power and consistency by hitting 14 home runs by mid-June. That total was more four-baggers than he had ever hit in any previous full season. A switch-hitter, Caminiti gets most of his homers when he bats against right-handed pitchers.

During the off season of 1994 (that unfortunately began in August), Caminiti was traded by the Astros to the San Diego Padres. In December of that year he was part of a huge 12-player deal that was the largest mass migration of ball players in decades. It may seem strange that a player like Caminiti should be dealt away. After all, he had hit 18 homers, driven in 75 runs, and posted a .283 batting average in the 115-game '94 season to help Houston climb to within a half game of the division leading Cincinnati Reds. But the deal was in keeping with the mean spirit of the times. The motivation for trading Caminiti was to pare down the Astros' payroll, a move that is certain to make the club's accountants a lot happier than its fans.

NEW YORK METS

OFP # **50**

First Report ☐

FREE AGENT PLAYER REPORT

Supplemental ☒

Date of Last Report

Player **CAMINITI** **KENNETH**
(LAST NAME) (FIRST NAME) (MIDDLE NAME)

Nickname

Home Address _____ Street _____ City _____ State _____ Zip Code

Home Phone ( )
Area Code

School Address _____ Street _____ City _____ State _____ Zip Code

School Phone ( )
Area Code

Position: **3B** Bats **S** Throws **R** Hgt. **6-0** Wgt. **185** D.O.B. _____

Team Name: **SAN JOSE STATE** City: **SAN JOSE** State: **CA**

Date Eligible: **6** MONTH **84** YEAR Regular ☒ Secondary ☐ Grad. Date **6/85**

Total Games Seen to Date: **3** Total Innings Pitched ☐ DATE LAST GAME SEEN **4/3/84**

RATING KEY	POSITION PLAYERS	Pres.	Fut.	PITCHERS	Pres.	Fut.	NON-PHYSICAL QUALITIES	
8–Outstanding	Hitting Ability	4	6	Fast Ball Vel.			Aggressiveness	
7–Very Good	Raw Power	5	5	Fast Ball Mvmt.			Drive	
6–Above Average	Power Frequency	4	5	Curve Ball			Self-Confidence	
5–Average	Running Speed	3	3	Slider			Mental Toughness	
4–Below Average	Base Running 4.5-4.4	3	3	Change-Up			Pressure Player	
3–Weak	Arm Strength	6	6	Other			Courage	
2–Poor	Arm Accuracy	5	6	Overall Control			Dedication	
	Fielding	4	5	Command			Coachability	
Use Major League	Range	5	5	Poise			Work Habits	
Grading Standards.	B. B. Instinct	6	6	B. B. Instinct			Off Field Habits	
Do Not Use Plusses	(TYPE OF HITTER)			DELIVERY			OVERALL MAKEUP GRADE	
or Minuses.	Pwr___ Linedrive___ Slap___			OH___ H 3/4 ___ L 3/4 ___ SA ___ UH ___				

PHYSICAL DESCRIPTION & INJURIES: Glasses ☐ Contacts ☐ Married: ☐ Yes ☐ No
MUSCULAR THIGHS-ARMS AND ACROSS BACK. DISLOCATED LEFT
SHOULDER EARLY IN YR.

STRENGTHS: Gd. ARM HITTING POTENTIAL WITH POWER POTENTIAL
VERY AGG WITH BAT AND IN THE FIELD. MAKES SLOW HIT PLAY
Gd.

WEAKNESSES: B.A. RUNNER

OVERALL SUMMATION: MAY HAVE QUICKER STROKE L.H. BUT MORE OF
POWER STROKE FROM R. SIDE. HARD NOSED GAMER. LOVE THE WAY HE
PLAYS COULD DEVELOP BETTER POWER THAN I GAVE HIM.

SIGNABILITY DATA: Asking for $ ☐ Actual Worth 30,000 Agent Involved Yes ☐ No ☐

START AT WHAT LEVEL: ☐

PROSPECT CATEGORY: Excellent ☐ Good ☐ Average ☒ Fringe ☐ Org. ☐ N.P. ☐

SCOUT'S NAME: **HARRY MINOR** Date **4/17/84**
WHITE - Office Copy YELLOW - Supervisors Copy PINK - Scouts Copy

ROD CAREW

ROD CAREW

*Y*oung people have little patience for listening to their elders' stories about "the Good Old Days." You want to sit through some
old geezer's recollections of how he won World War II in the Quarter-
master Corps? Or how great our cities used to be? Or how you once
could eat anything you wanted and not be afraid you were killing yourself? No.

But when it comes to baseball nostalgia, most young people are a
willing audience. If you doubt it, look at the attendance for Old Timers
Day games at major league parks.

So when a scout talks of the days before the major league draft
system was introduced in 1965, it's worth your time to listen. And
because he does it with some wistfulness, we get a sense of what was
lost to get what we now have.

Scouting before 1965 was much more a "seat of the pants" operation than it is today. Thirty years ago, when a scout saw a prospect, it was a closely guarded secret. There was no Major League Scouting Bureau that would report on a kid for all the teams to see. Back then, when a scout found a prospect he cultivated the kid and his folks, haggled about the money, and then signed him. That was it.

For an insight into what scouting was like before the draft, the person to talk to is Herb Stein, a veteran scout with the Minnesota Twins who has been beating the bushes for over thirty-five years. Of all the thousands of players he's seen and the hundreds that he's signed, one stands out above the rest: Rod Carew.

In 1964 the son of a friend of Herb's was a student at George Washington High School in Manhattan. He knew about a young Panamanian who was working out with the school team. He told Herb about him. When Herb saw him play, he knew this kid was something very special.

At the time, Rod wasn't eligible due to some academic confusion about his academic credits from Panama. That proved to be a big break for Stein: If Carew couldn't play high school ball, very few other scouts would have a chance to watch him.

Stein knew that Carew had joined a sandlot team, the Bronx Cavaliers, and was playing on ball fields that you needed a compass to find. Week after week Stein watched Carew, and each week he became more convinced that this kid could be a baseball scout's equivalent of the Holy Grail—a great ballplayer. Soon, Stein and Carew struck up a friendship.

But even in those days, secrets were hard to keep. Somehow the White Sox, Tigers, and Red Sox learned about him, but luckily for Stein, their scouts never seemed to be around. Until one Sunday; the very Sunday that Herb decided to show off this talent to his boss, the director of Twins' Player Personnel, Hal Keller. Stein was shocked to see scouts from the other three teams sitting in the stands. Stein was not a happy man.

When they told Herb that they were there to scout a ballplayer named Harry Greenfield, Stein became convinced then and there that not only is there a God but that He is a Twins fan. Now Stein's job was to get the other scouts out of there before the game started so they wouldn't see Carew play. Stein knew that Greenfield was playing somewhere. Just where he wasn't sure, but he wanted these guys as far away from Carew as possible. He said he believed that the kid was playing in Yonkers that afternoon and, being a nice guy, even gave them directions to the ballpark. They may still be looking for it.

That day Carew got seven hits in a doubleheader and Hal Keller said, "Sign that kid."

In those days there were some rules about signing. Teams had to wait until midnight of the day the high school prospect graduated before they could sign him. Stein arranged for a dinner with Carew and his parents at a Bronx restaurant to celebrate Rod's graduation. With one eye on the clock—it was about nine at night when they sat down—Stein just kept talking. Three long hours later it was midnight and time to get down to business.

Remember that this was 1964 and the days of huge salaries were some twenty years in the future. So Stein offered Carew what he felt was a fair price at that time, $5,000. In addition to that bonus for signing, he proposed a Class A contract for $400 a month with an incentive bonus if Carew advanced through the minors. The total package could net him $7,500 plus his salary. The figure seems ludicrous today because if Carew were still playing he'd earn more than that each time he came up to bat.

Even though Carew was only eighteen, he showed his maturity by handling the negotiations himself. He said that he wanted forty-eight hours to think it over. So, Stein started talking again, telling him about the Minnesota organization and the opportunities it offered. Carew listened and then said that he still wanted some time. But to a scout trying to sign a prospect, time is the enemy.

Stein had hidden the kid pretty well and he didn't want him shopping himself around for a better deal. But what could he do? Then Stein got an inspiration. He figured that it was time to let someone else do the talking, and that someone was an assistant scout for the Chicago White Sox.

Stein knew that the head scout of the Sox, Dutch Daitch, was out of town and that his assistant couldn't make any offer without his boss's approval. So Stein said to Rod, "Call the White Sox scout and ask him what he'll offer you. If he doesn't offer you more than I have, you sign with me. If he beats me, you're a White Sox." Rod agreed and Stein gave him the guy's number and a fistful of coins.

Carew reached the assistant scout and told him about Stein's offer. Herb watched as Rod listened intently and his heart jumped when he saw Rod's face drop. Stein knew that the assistant couldn't make any commitment, and when the assistant asked Rod to wait for a few days, Rod thanked him and told him that he was signing with the Twins.

By the convergence of the three great forces that shape successful scouting— insight, perseverance, and luck—Stein won the service of one of the greatest ballplayers of the modern era. Carew went on to win the AL Batting Championship seven times and was MVP in 1977. Unquestionably the proudest moment of Stein's career was in 1991, when he and his wife were in Cooperstown to watch Rod Carew inducted into the Baseball Hall of Fame.

MINNESOTA TWINS BASEBALL CLUB

EXECUTIVE OFFICES ◆ **PHONE: 884–4031** ◆ **TICKET OFFICE**

METROPOLITAN **STADIUM** • **BLOOMINGTON,** **MINNESOTA** **55420**

1964 Scouting Report

Rodney Cline Carew 2B BL-TR 6-170

Address: 535 West 151st. St. New York City 10031

Date of Birth: 10-01-1945

Tele: TO2 2573

Father: Eric   Mother Olga

School: George Washington H.S. Grad. class June 1964

Place of Birth: Gatun, Panama

The following report on player Rod Carew covers a period between April 1964 and June 1964. His graduating class is June 24, 1964.

I have seen this boy in a number of games during this period, and the following evaluation is submitted. Physically he has a fine body, wiry type. He has no known injuries or physical defects. He has good hands, reflexes and range. His movements and actions are good. He is knowledgeable and has shown good baseball instincts, which is rare among young players. He makes the double play, but he needs help shifting his feet and getting rid of the ball quicker. He also takes too much time getting rid of the ball to first base. It looks like he challenges the runner, and his throw just beats the runner by a step. He is a quiet and nonchalant player, but he does the job.

He is an excellent runner. Goes to 1B in 4 seconds and on a bunt he does 3.8 seconds. His base running is very good, and he runs with very little effort. Gets good jump on pitcher when stealing.

He has a major league arm at 2B. He was worked out at SS, but did not have the arm strength at that position.

He is a good hitter. Can hit the ball to all fields. He has strong arms and great wrist action. He has a quick bat. On contact the ball jumps off his bat. He can hit an inside pitch to left field and make good contact. He has also shown good power. I have seen him hit balls 400 feet. He also has a good idea of the strike zone.

Not many clubs know about him. I have seen him play a lot of games, and the only scouts I have seen were: Detroit, Boston, White Sox. He did not play High School ball. He could only be seen in sandlot ball.

In summing up, this boy has great potential. The projection on him in pro ball is good. Once in pro ball if he can get use to being away from home, accepting the good and bad, and the many adversities in this game, he will become one hell of a player.

Monetary considerations: I am prepared to offer this boy a cash bonus of $5000.00, Incentive Bonus Plan, and $400.00 per month. My relationship with him is good, and have good chance of signing him.

Herb Stein

ROGER CLEMENS

ROGER CLEMENS

O ne month before Clemens was picked by the Red Sox in the first round of the June 1983 draft, the Mets took another look at him.

The New York club had chosen Clemens in the twelfth round of the 1981 draft when he was playing at San Jacinto J.C. in Texas. But you can't get rich on the bonus money that clubs pay to twelfth-round draft choices, so Clemens turned down an offer to sign with the Mets and went to the University of Texas instead, thereby freeing himself for a later draft. (Incidentally, the player the Mets selected in the thirteenth round that year was Lenny Dykstra.)

By 1983 Clemens was free to be drafted again, and after being passed up by nineteen other clubs, he went to Boston. That year he split the season between Winter Haven and New Britain, where he had a combined 7–2 won-loss record and a 1.33 ERA. In 1984 Clemens started at Pawtucket and was brought up to the Sox during the season. The 1985 season was a disappointment to Sox fans as their club had an 81–81 record and finished fifth in the AL East. Clemens was the fifth man in the Red Sox rotation that year. But the following season, 1986, was a totally different story. Clemens took over and won twenty-four games while losing only four and led the Sox into the World Series. Young Lochinvar from out of the (South) West had arrived in Beantown.

Clemens fanned twenty Mariners on April 29, 1986 to set a major league record for strikeouts in a single game. That year he was the AL MVP and won the first of his three Cy Young Awards. Clemens has been the league leader with the lowest ERA four times, his best being in 1990, when he had an unhittable 1.93 ERA. Clemens throws a lot harder than the Mets thought he could, and his control is deadly accurate. A measure of Clemens' effectiveness is his amazing strikeouts-to-bases-on-balls ratio. Whereas a strikeout artist like Nolan Ryan has 2.04, Steve Carlton 2.26, and Bert Blyleven 2.8, Clemens has over 3 to 1.

In 1993 arm trouble plagued Clemens, resulting in his first losing season, but he returned to form for the Red Sox in 1994. As all scouts say, "Sometimes you miss one." The Mets missed Roger Clemens in more ways than one.

NEW YORK METS

OFP # 55

First Report ☐

FREE AGENT PLAYER REPORT

Supplemental ☒

Date of Last Report

Player | CLEMENS | ROGER |
(LAST NAME) (FIRST NAME) (MIDDLE NAME)

Nickname

Home Address _____
Street   City   State   Zip Code

Home Phone ( )
Area Code

School Address _____
Street   City   State   Zip Code

School Phone ( )
Area Code

Position: RHP   Bats R   Throws R   Hgt. 6-3   Wgt. 205   D.O.B.

Team Name: UNIV. OF TEXAS   City: AUSTIN   State: TE

Date Eligible: 6   83   Regular ☒   Secondary ☐   Grad. Date 6/84
MONTH YEAR

Total Games Seen to Date: 1   Total Innings Pitched 9   DATE LAST GAME SEEN 5/15/83

RATING KEY	POSITION PLAYERS	Pres.	Fut.	PITCHERS	Pres.	Fut.	NON-PHYSICAL QUALITIES	
8–Outstanding	Hitting Ability			Fast Ball Vel.	5	6	Aggressiveness	
7–Very Good	Raw Power			Fast Ball Mvmt.	4	5	Drive	
6–Above Average	Power Frequency			Curve Ball	4	5	Self-Confidence	
5–Average	Running Speed			Slider	4	5	Mental Toughness	
4–Below Average	Base Running			Change-Up	0	0	Pressure Player	
3–Weak	Arm Strength			Other	0	0	Courage	
2–Poor	Arm Accuracy			Overall Control	4	5	Dedication	
	Fielding			Command	5	5	Coachability	
Use Major League	Range			Poise	5	5	Work Habits	
Grading Standards.	B. B. Instinct			B. B. Instinct	5	5	Off Field Habits	
Do Not Use Plusses	(TYPE OF HITTER)			DELIVERY			OVERALL MAKEUP GRADE	
or Minuses.	Pwr____ Linedrive____ Slap____			OH___ H 3/4 _X_ L 3/4 ___ SA ___ UH ___				

PHYSICAL DESCRIPTION & INJURIES: Glasses ☐   Contacts ☐   Married: ☐ Yes ☐ No

GOOD STRONG PITCHERS BODY.

STRENGTHS: HAS A GOOD ARM. FAST BALL HAD AVG VEL. MOST OF THE GAME WAS 87-90 IN 1ST 2 INNINGS WAS 85-87 TILL THE END. CURVE HAS GD ROTATION. SLIDER WAS SHARP EARLY IN GAME.

WEAKNESSES: CONTROL WAS ONLY FAIR. DIDN'T SEE A STRAIGHT CHANGE. FAST BALL DOESN'T HAVE MUCH MOVEMENT WHEN IN STRIKE ZONE

OVERALL SUMMATION: USED SLIDER SPARINGLY. COULD BE A GOOD PITCH FOR HIM. DIDN'T THROW ANY AFTER 4TH INNING. COULD USE A CHANGE OF PACE PITCH

SIGNABILITY DATA: Asking for $ _____   Actual Worth _____   Agent Involved   Yes ☐   No ☐

START AT WHAT LEVEL: _____

PROSPECT CATEGORY: Excellent ☐   Good ☒   Average ☐   Fringe ☐   Org. ☐   N.P. ☐

SCOUT'S NAME: HARRY MINOR   Date 5/16/83

WHITE - Office Copy   YELLOW - Supervisors Copy   PINK - Scouts Copy

RON
DARLING   P

RON DARLING

When a scout goes shopping for talent, he usually doesn't wind up watching Ivy League baseball games. After all, up until 1981, only two players from the league known more for brains than base hits had ever been chosen as first round draft picks. In 1974 Bill Almon from Brown was selected by the Padres. Mike Stenhouse from Harvard was the first-round choice of Oakland in 1979. Stenhouse didn't sign with the A's, sat out the season, and was selected by Montreal in the following year's draft. Both Almon and Stenhouse had forgettable major league careers.

So a trip to the hallowed halls of academia is not high on a scout's list of priorities. But in 1981 there was a prospect up at New Haven who scouts felt was worth a look. Ron Darling was now a pitcher with Yale, although he had been a shortstop on his St. John's High School team in Worcester, Mass. Take a look at what the scouts reported.

The year before, Darling had had a great season for Old Eli with an 11–2 record and a 1.31 ERA. But a year later, the year the above report was written, he spread himself too thin. When he wasn't pitching, he played the field. The result was that Darling wound up with a so-so 9–4 mark. But he redeemed his entire season with his performance in a 1981 NCAA playoff game. Had the Royals' scout been there, Kansas City very likely would have chosen Darling as their first pick instead of selecting outfielder Dave Leeper, who had a career .075 BA in his forty plate appearances.

In the college playoffs Darling engaged in a classic pitching duel against St. John's University ace, Frank Viola. That day, both pitchers showed their big league potential. Both Darling and Viola shut out the opposition for eleven innings. Darling had struck out 16 batters and had a no-hitter going. In the twelfth a scratch single and some porous defensive play by Yale gave St. John's the victory.

The Texas Rangers were so impressed with Darling they made him their number one choice in the June draft. Viola was picked second by the Minnesota Twins. In 1982 Darling was traded to the Mets, where he stayed for seven seasons, compiling a 99–72 record before going to Oakland in '91.

MAJOR LEAGUE SCOUTING BUREAU
FREE AGENT REPORT

Overall future potential __66.0__

Report No. __1__

PLAYER __DARLING, JR.__ __RONALD__ __MAURICE__ Position __RHP__
Last name · First name · Middle name

Current Address _____

City

Telephone _____ Date of Birth _____ Ht. ____ Wt. ____ Bats _R_ Throws _R_
(Area Code)

Permanent address (if different from above) _____

Team Name __YALE U.__ City __NEW HAVEN__ State __CONN.__

Scout __D. BOGARD__ Date _____ Race __WHITE__ Games __1__ Innings _____

RATING KEY	NON-PITCHERS		Pres.	Fut.	PITCHERS		Pres.	Fut.	USE WORD DESCRIPTION
8–Outstanding	Hitting Ability	*			Fast Ball	*	6	6	Habits _____
7–Very Good	Power	*			Curve	*	6	7	Dedication _____
6–Above Average	Running Speed	*			Control		5	6	Agility _____
5–Average	Base Running				Change of Pace		0	0	Aptitude _____
4–Below Average	Arm Strength	*			Slider	*	6	6	Phys. Maturity __good__
3–Well Below Average	Arm Accuracy				Knuckle Ball		0	0	Emot. Maturity __good__
2–Poor	Fielding	*			Other	*	0	0	Married _____
	Range				Poise		5	6	
Use One Grade	Baseball Instinct				Baseball Instinct		5	6	Date Eligible
Grade On Major	Aggressiveness				Aggressiveness		5	5	06-82
League Standards	Pull Str. Away	Opp. Field			Arm Action __good__				Phase
Not Amateur					Delivery __good__				Reg.

Physical Description (Injuries, Glasses, etc.) GRADUATION __06-82__

TALL, WELL PROP. BUILD.

Abilities

EFFORTLESS, DECEPTIVE DEL. AB. AVE. VEL. ON TAILING, SINKING FB
TIGHT, BITING ROT. ON CB. HARD, SWEEPING SL. POT. TO
HAVE AB. AVG. COMMAND.

Weaknesses

LANDS ON STIFF FRONT LEG, BUT GETS OVER IT WELL.

Summation and Signability Worth ~~_____~~
GOOD ATHLETE, HAS FEEL FOR PITCHING, HAS THE STUFF AND
POISE NOW. COULD COME QUICK.

KANSAS CITY ROYALS

FREE AGENT REPORT

METS — TEXAS — OAK

Overall future potential ___66___   Report No. _1_

PLAYER __DARLING__ (Last name) __RONALD__ (First name) __MAURICE__ (Middle name) Position _RHP_

Current Address __YALE STATION BOX 204__ __NEW HAVEN__ (City) __CT.__ (State) __06520__ (Zip Code)

Telephone __203-452-1346__ (Area Code) Date of Birth _8/19/60_ Ht. _6:3_ Wt. _205_ Bats _R_ Throws _R_

Permanent address (if different from above) __19 WOODLAND ST. MILLBURY, MA - 01527__

Team Name __YALE UNIV.__ City __NEW HAVEN__ State __CT__

Scout __TOM FERRICK__ Date _____ Race __OTHER__ Games _1_ Innings _7_

RATING KEY	NON-PITCHERS		Pres.	Fut.	PITCHERS		Pres.	Fut.	USE WORD DESCRIPTION	
8–Outstanding	Hitting Ability	*			Fast Ball	*	5	6	Habits	Good
7–Very Good	Power	*			Curve	*	5	5	Dedication	FAIR
6–Above Average	Running Speed	*			Control		4	5	Agility	V GOOD
5–Average	Base Running				Change of Pace		–	–	Aptitude	GOOD
4–Below Average	Arm Strength	*			Slider	*	5	5	Phys. Maturity	V GOOD
3–Well Below Average	Arm Accuracy				Knuckle Ball				Emot. Maturity	GOOD
2–Poor	Fielding	*			Other	*			Married	NO
	Range				Poise		5	5		
Use One Grade	Baseball Instinct				Baseball Instinct		5	5	Date Eligible	JUNE '81
Grade On Major	Aggressiveness				Aggressiveness		5	5		
League Standards	Pull Str. Away Opp. Field				Arm Action	GOOD			Phase	REG.
Not Amateur					Delivery	GOOD				

Physical Description (Injuries, Glasses, etc.) GRADUATION___6/82___

CONTACTS. GOOD PITCHERS BODY. COORDINATION - RHYTHM BODY
CONTROL GOOD. N/34 SLOT SOMEWHAT STRAIGHT UP AT FINISH
OF DELIVERY.

Abilities BODY SIZE AND ARM EXCELLENT. MOVES WITH QUICKNESS.
TO 1B. FB IN THIS ONE LOOK RANGED FROM 4-5-6. BASICALLY
5 M.L. FB WITH SOME 6 M.L. FB. SLIDER 5 M.L. CURVE (A SLOW
CURVE) GOOD COMMAND OF IT. CONTROL FAIR M.L.

Weaknesses NOT OVERLY AGGRESSIVE ON MOUND. A LITTLE LACKADAISICAL
ATTITUDE. ACTED A LITTLE BORED AT TIMES. BUT HIS TALENT
OVERCAME THIS ATTITUDE. MIGHT HAVE TO BE MOTIVATED AT
TIMES.

Summation and Signability FINE EQUIPMENT FOR FRONT LINE M.L
STARTER. SHOULD GO HIGH IN M.L. DRAFT. 1ST ROUND

DELINO DeSHIELDS

*I*t would be difficult to say which of DeShields's statistics as a senior in high school was more impressive. As a star basketball player he averaged 21 points a game. As a shortstop he hit .355. But when you're 5'10", your chances of making it in pro basketball, where the guards can be 6'8", don't look too promising. And if it means passing up a scholarship at Villanova in order to play pro baseball, so be it. DeShields, who was Montreal's first choice in the 1987 draft, signed on with the Expos and within four years established himself as a bona fide major leaguer. (The Royals, who were obviously impressed by DeShields, used their first pick on Kevin Appier.)

A look at DeShields's record shows that he was less effective as a minor leaguer than as a player in the majors. His BA from '87 through '89 in the minors was .252. In his first four years in the majors, DeShields hit .277. Talk about learning on the job!

DeShields made a seismic impact in his debut with Montreal. On April 9, 1990, he collected four hits in his first game. He wound up batting .289 that season. The following year DeShields fell prey to the sophomore jinx when he hit .238 and led the NL in strikeouts with 151. In 1992 he regained his earlier form and batted .292 and cut down his strikeouts by over 30 percent from the previous year. The following season he struck out only sixty-four times, less than half of his '91 strikeout total.

After batting .295 for the Expos in 1993, DeShields was traded to Los Angeles in what was for Expos fans a very chancy trade for Pedro J. Martinez. Montreal gave up one of the league's best lead-off batters in a season in which realignment brought the Expos and the Atlanta Braves into the same division.

But unlike most trades, this one worked for both teams. DeShields, although on the DL early in 1994 with a broken cheekbone, recovered and was a dependable number two hitter behind Brett Butler. Together they helped the Dodgers wind up in first place in the West, 3$^{1}/_{2}$ games ahead of the Giants when the season died of greed.

Pedro J. Martinez, one of the fourteen Martinezes in the majors that year, won eleven games as the Expos shocked the favored Braves in the East. Montreal led Atlanta by six games before the curtain descended on Major League Baseball in August 1994.

KANSAS CITY ROYALS
FREE AGENT REPORT

Overall Future Potential _____ 67

Nat'l. Double Check   Yes __✓__ No_____

Scout's Report # _____1_____   Scout _FERRICK_

PLAYER _DESHIELDS_ _DELANO_ _L_   Pos. _SS_   Date _4/25/87_
    Last Name   First Name   Middle Initial

School or Team _SEAFORD H.S._   City and State _SEAFORD, DE_

Permanent Address _____

Current Address _____

Date of Birth _1/15/87_ Ht. _6.2_ Wt. _180_ Bats _L_ Throws _R_ DATE ELIGIBLE _JUNE 87_ PHASE _R_

Game Date(s) _APR. 23 '87_ Games _____1_____ Innings _10_ Graduation _JUNE '87_

OFFICE USE
Report No. _____
Player No. _____

No.	RATING KEY	M.P.H.	NON-PITCHERS	Pres.	Fut.	PITCHERS	Pres.	Fut.	MAKEUP
8	Outstanding	94-	Hitting Ability	4	6	Fast Ball			
7	Very Good	91-93	Power	3	4	Life of Fastball			
6	Above Average	88-90	Running Speed	8	8	Curve			
5	Average	85-87	Base Running	5	6	Control			
4	Below Average	82-84	Arm Strength	6	6	Change of Pace			
3	Well Below Ave.	79-81	Arm Accuracy	5	6	Slider			
2	Poor	0-78	Fielding	5	6	Other			
			Range	5	6	Poise			

MAKEUP	Ex.	Good	Fair	Poor
Habits	4	3	2	1
Dedication	4	3	2	1
Agility	4	3	2	1
Aptitude	4	3	2	1
Phys. Mat.	4	3	2	1
Emot. Mat.	4	3	2	1
Baseball Inst.	4	3	2	1
Aggressiveness	4	3	2	1
OVERALL	4	3	2	1

USE ONE GRADE
Grade On
Major League
Standard

Hitting: (✓)
Pull ....3 ____
St. Away ....2 ✓
Opp. Field.. 1 ____
   3.9

	EX	GOOD	FAIR	POOR
Running Time To 1st Base				
Arm Action	4	3	2	1
	3/4	OH	SIDE	OTHER
Delivery	4	3	2	1

Gun Reading _____ to _____ MPH

Physical Description (Injuries, Glasses, etc.) NO GLASSES. NO KNOWN INJURIES. ROUGH WITH BODY. GOOD ATHLETIC BODY. VILLANOVA BASKETBALL RECRUIT. HAS SIGNED LETTER OF INTENT. FAIR GRADES.

Abilities GOOD ATHLETE. FLUID ACTIONS - GOOD HANDS. AGILE + QUICK + QUIETLY HARD NOSED. AGGRESSIVE ON BASES. NOT AFRAID OF CONTACT - NO FEAR AT PLATE. GOOD BAT SPEED + GOOD BAT MECHANICS. ALSO QUICK FEET. INSTINCTS GOOD ON BASES.

Weaknesses JUST NEEDS PLAYING TIME - AND INSTRUCTION ON FIELD-ING TECHNIQUES

Signability: Ex._____ Good_____ Fair __✓__ Poor_____ Worth: $ _75-100,000_
FAMILY AT POVERTY LEVEL + NO FATHER AROUND - MOTHER ALCOHOLIC LIVING WITH RELATIVES. VILLANOVA IN PICTURE BUT MONEY + PRO BASEBALL NOW WILL BE A BIG FACTOR.

Makeup Evaluation and Player Summation GOOD ATHLETE. WILL BE ABLE TO PLAY SS. IN ML. HAS ENOUGH RAW SKILLS TO BE A GOOD ML SS. GOOD BAT POTENTIAL. LC + REF GOT POWER.

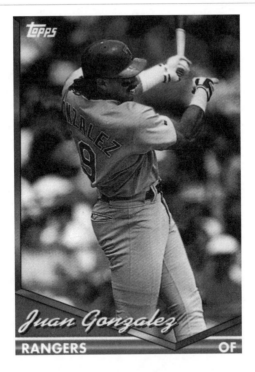

RANGERS OF

JUAN GONZALEZ

*I*f you look at Juan Gonzalez's scouting report too quickly you may overlook one very interesting number. It's next to the abbreviation, "Wt." It shows 175 pounds. That was then. Today, Juan Gonzalez weighs 215 pounds. He's put on forty pounds of pure muscle since he started in organized ball in 1986.

The Texas Rangers didn't draft Gonzalez, but they signed him as a free agent because at that time Puerto Rico was not included in the draft. Gonzalez's first season performance was nothing to base a movie on. In 60 games he didn't hit one out of the park and batted a very modest .240. The only department he led the Gulf Coast League in was outfield errors. Things could only get better. And after all, Juan was still growing.

At Gastonia in the South Atlantic League the following season, Gonzalez raised his BA to .265 and he started to find the range. He hit 14 home runs and 21 doubles. But 1988 wasn't very kind to Gonzalez as he struggled in the Florida State League at Charlotte, where he hit only 8 home runs and batted .256. He was also on the DL for almost two months. The next year, Gonzalez started strong and since then he has never looked back. His swing became grooved and the awesomeness of his power became manifest. He hit 21 homers and had 85 RBIs at Tulsa in the Texas League and in 1990, Gonzalez led the American Association in home runs with 29 and RBIs with 101; he was called up by the Rangers at the end of the season.

In 1991 he started to feast on American League pitching. He hit 27 homers and knocked in 102 runs in what was only a preview of things to come. In 1992 he led the AL with 43 homers and 109 RBIs, and in 1993 repeated with a league-leading 46 round trippers. He had 118 RBIs and hit .310, the highest average he had ever attained, including his years in the minors.

The common wisdom around baseball used to be that catching is the toughest position to play. Well, maybe. But could there possibly be a tougher position than pitching when you're only 60 feet 6 inches away from Juan Gonzalez, who, if he doesn't hit one out of sight, might just hit one through your entire body?

TEXAS RANGERS
FREE AGENT REPORT

Overall future potential __66__   Report No. __1__

PLAYER __GONZALEZ__   __JUAN__   __ALBERTO__   Position __OF__
     Last name   First name   Middle name

Current Address __URB. CATONI NO. 9 VIEGA BAJA__   __P.R.__
                        City   State   Zip Code

Telephone __809-858-2167__ Date of Birth __10-16-69__ Ht. __6'3__ Wt. __175__ Bats __R__ Throws __R__
     (Area Code)

Permanent address (if different from above) _____

Team Name __BAYAMON__   City __BAYAMON__   State __PUERTO RICO__

Scout __LUIS ROSA__   Date __1/10/86__ Race __HISPCAU__ Games __7__ Innings _____

RATING KEY	NON-PITCHERS		Pres.	Fut.	PITCHERS		Pres.	Fut.	USE WORD DESCRIPTION
8–Outstanding	Hitting Ability	*	4	6	Fast Ball	*			Habits _EXCL_
7–Very Good	Power	*	4	6	Curve	*			Dedication _EXCL_
6–Above Average	Running Speed		5	5	Control				Agility _GOOD_
5–Average	Base Running	60yds	7	0	Change of Pace				Aptitude _GOOD_
4–Below Average	Arm Strength	*	6	7	Slider	*			Phys. Maturity _AVG_
3–Well Below Average	Arm Accuracy		5	5	Knuckle Ball				Emot. Maturity _AVG_
2–Poor	Fielding	*	5	6	Other	*			Married _NO_
	Range		6	6	Poise				
Use One Grade	Baseball Instinct		5	5	Baseball Instinct				Date Eligible
Grade On Major	Aggressiveness		6	6	Aggressiveness				_5/86_
League Standards	Pull Str. Away	Opp. Field			Arm Action _____				Phase
Not Amateur	_____ ✓	_____			Delivery _____				

Physical Description (Injuries, Glasses, etc.)   GRADUATION __5/87__

TALL-WIRY-STRONG-GROWING BOY- NO KNOWN INJURIES
OR PHYSICAL HANDICAPS

Abilities GOOD ALL AROUND PLAYER- HAS POWER- AGGR. HITTER
GOOD FIELDER- GETS GOOD JUMP ON BALL-STRONG ARM
SWINGS HARD AT EVERY PITCH. BEST OF PROSPECT ON ISLAND.
GOOD MAKE-UP- DETERMINED PLAYER. GIVES 100%+ ALL
THE TIME.

Weaknesses
JUST NEEDS TO PLAY! RUNNING NEEDS TO BE
IMPROVED.

Summation and Signability   Worth _____ + INCENTIVE + SCHOOL

PREMIUM PLAYER- COST MONEY DUE TO HIGH DEMAND.
COULD BE ONE OF BEST PLAYERS I HAVE SIGNED.

DWIGHT GOODEN

*I*n 1982 when Mets scout Joe McIlvaine saw Gooden pitch for his Hillsborough High School team in Tampa, he almost fell out of the stands. Could this kid be the replacement for Tom Seaver, whom the Mets had dealt to Cincinnati five years before in an ill-advised and colossally unpopular move? Since Seaver's departure, the Mets had seemingly suffered a New York version of the Red Sox Babe Ruth curse. The team had finished in last place three times and next-to-last twice in the NL East since Tom Terrific was sent packing. Could Gooden be the one to break the spell? Maybe, just maybe. The Mets, who went fifth in the first round of the 1982 draft, grabbed Gooden after the Cubs, Blue Jays, Padres, and Twins had passed him up.

Right from the start the Mets were lucky with Gooden. Instead of the projected $95,000 that McIlvaine thought it would take to get him, the Mets signed Gooden for a $60,000 bonus. He went to Kingsport that year and was promoted to Lynchburg in the Carolina League in 1983. There Gooden went 19–4 and led the league in wins, ERA, shutouts, and strikeouts. The heir-apparent to Seaver was ready. In his first season in the majors with the Mets, in 1984, he won seventeen games and led the NL with 276 strikeouts, an average of over 1.2 per inning, and he easily won Rookie of the Year honors.

The Seaver curse had been broken, and the Mets finished second in the NL East in 1985. That year Gooden's twenty-four wins, his astounding 1.53 ERA, sixteen complete games and 268 strikeouts led the league in those departments and he won the Cy Young Award. The following season Gooden's pitching propelled the Mets to the top of the NL East for the first time in thirteen years. Although he has had only one season in which he won twenty games, Gooden has a lifetime won–loss percentage of .655 that ties him with Sandy Koufax.

Arm trouble has made the past three years an anxious time for both Gooden and the Mets. Since 1991 he has won an average of eleven games a year, and in '92 and '93 Gooden experienced his only losing seasons. A freak toe injury put him on the DL for the third time in his career in 1994.

Although Gooden is acknowledged as one of the great pitchers of our time, he has never won a postseason game in four All-Star games, two Championship Series, and one World Series.

Gooden's suspension for the entire 1995 season for repeated drug use greatly tarnished his former luster with Mets fans.

☒ First Report   **NEW YORK METS**

☐ Supplemental   **FREE AGENT PLAYER REPORT**

Player: **GOODEN** (LAST NAME)   **DWIGHT** (FIRST NAME)   (MIDDLE NAME)   Position **R** **P**

Current Address .... City .... State .... Zip

Telephone .... Date of Birth **□□□□□** Ht. **6' 4"** Wt. **190** Bats **R** Throws **R**
(MONTH) (DAY) (YEAR)   (L.R.S.)   (LR)

Permanent Home Address (If different from above) ....
(STREET NUMBER)   (CITY)   (STATE)

Team Category **HS**   School **HILLSBOROUGH HS** City **TAMPA** State **FLA** **JUNE 1982**
(HS • LG • JC • CL • AM • OT)   (GRAD. DATE & YEAR)

Team Name .... City .... State .... Race **B**
(IF OTHER THAN HS • JC • CL)

Scout **Jo McIlvaine**   (NAME)   **115** (NO.)   Date **053082** (MONTH) (DAY) (YEAR)   CUMULATIVE TOTALS   Games **1** Innings **5**

Date Eligible **JUNE 1982**
Phase **REG**
Prior Draft: Last Club ....
Year .... No. ....
Should We Draft? **YES**

Prospect Rating
☒ Definite
☐ Chance
☐ N.P.
Signed by ....

Status
☒ Double Check
☐ 2nd Double Check
☐ Will Follow

USE WORD DESCRIPTION
MENTAL MAKEUP ....
Habits ....
Dedication ....
Agility **EXCELLENT**
Physical Maturity **GOOD**
Military ....
Married **NO**

RATING KEY	NON-PITCHERS	Pres.	Fut.	PITCHERS	Pres.	Fut.
8—Outstanding	Hitting Ability			Fast Ball	**5**	**5**
7—Very Good	Power			Curve	**4**	**6**
6—Above Average	Running Speed			Control	**4**	**5**
5—Average	Base Running			Change of Pace		
4—Below Average	Arm Strength			Slider		
3—Well Below Average	Arm Accuracy			Knuckle Ball		
2—Poor	Fielding			Fielding	**5**	**6**
1—Very Poor	Range			Poise	**4**	**5**
Use One Grade	Baseball Instinct			Baseball Instinct	**5**	**5**
Grade On Major	Aggressiveness			Aggressiveness	**6**	**6**
League Standards	Pull Str. Away Opp. Field			Arm Action **GOOD**		
Not Amateur	....			Delivery **GOOD**		

Fast Ball (cont.) Fut. **7**

Overall Evaluation / Future Potential **6** **4**

What's He Worth? **9** **5** (THOUSAND)

Will He Sign At Your Price?
☐ Yes
☐ No
☒ Don't Know

Physical Description (body, injuries, etc.) **GREAT PITCHER'S BODY - TALL WITH LONG ARMS + LEGS. LOOSE BODY, MUST FILL OUT AND ADD WEIGHT**

Eyes' Status: **NG**   **VERY AGILE AND GRACEFUL**

Strength **ARM STRENGTH. FB TAILS IN ON RH BATTERS. CB THROWN HARD WITH BITE. GOOD ATHLETE, AGILE, THROWS CAT LIKE ACTION OFF MOUND. BEST HS PITCHER IN FLA IN LAST 5 YRS. NOT MUCH EFFORT REQUIRED ON FB.**

Weaknesses: **THROWS ACROSS BODY. CB NEEDS MORE CONSISTENCY. NO CHG SHOWN. NEEDS EXCLUSIVE CONCENTRATION. TRIFLE LAZY. STARTS SIDESADDLE.**

Summation and Signability: **THERE IS NO TELLING HOW GOOD THIS YOUNG MAN COULD BE. ALL THE SIGNS FOR FUTURE IMPROVEMENT ARE PRESENT HERE PLUS AN A1 BODY. IN SCOUTING THE STATE OF FLA FOR 8 YEARS HE IS THE BEST LOOKING PITCHER PROSPECT I'VE SEEN FROM THE STATE IN ALL THESE YEARS. HE IS ALSO A POWERFUL HITTER AND CAN RUN. HE SHOULD NOT BE A TOUGH SIGN ALTHOUGH CUBS #1 DRAFT CHOICE IN 1981, VANCE LOVELACE CAME FROM SAME SCHOOL AND ASKED FOR A BUNDLE. A SUREFIRE ML DRAFT WHO SHOULD DEVELOP INTO A POWER PITCHER PAR EXCELLENCE. HE IS ONLY 17 YRS OLD. WILL PLAY HIS ENTIRE ROOKIE YR AT THIS AGE.**

COPY SENT TO

WILL SIGN.

TOMMY GREENE

W hen Greene became eligible for the major league draft in 1985, he was in fast company. Also up for the draft were future stars like Will Clark, Barry Larkin, Barry Bonds, Pete Incaviglia, Gregg Jefferies, and Rafael Palmeiro. The group was made up of mostly college players; only Greene and Jefferies were high schoolers. The Braves selected Greene as their first choice, but he saw only limited action with Atlanta before being traded to the Phillies in August 1990 along with Dale Murphy.

In 1991, his first full season in the majors, Greene posted an impressive 13–7 record and had the best ERA of the Phillies' starters with 3.38. On May 23, 1991, Greene pitched a no-hitter against Montreal, the first of two no-hitters pitched in the majors that year. The other was a perfect game by Dennis Martinez, then on the Expos.

In 1992 Greene was on the DL from mid-May until September and had a 3–3 mark in twelve starts.

Nineteen ninety-three was Greene's finest year. He won 16 games and lost 4 and was among the NL leaders in complete games with seven, strikeouts with 167 and won–loss percentage with .800. After splitting two decisions in the NL Championship Series against Atlanta that year, Greene was buffeted by the Blue Jays in the '93 World Series as they tagged him for seven hits and seven earned runs in $2\frac{1}{3}$ innings. In 1994, Greene spent more time on the DL and his control seemed to be eluding him.

As a batter, Greene has hit four home runs, two in 1991 when he drove in seven runs and two in 1993 when he had 10 RBIs.

KANSAS CITY ROYALS
FREE AGENT REPORT

OFFICE USE
Report No. _____
Player No. _____

Overall Future Potential __58__

Nat'l. Double Check Yes __✓__ No_____   Scout __FERRICK__

Scout's Report # __1__   Date __4/9/85__

PLAYER __GREENE__ (Last Name) __IRA__ (First Name) __TOMMY__ (Middle Initial)   TEAM NAME __WHITEVILLE HS__   Pos. __RHP__

Permanent Address _____ Street ____ City ____ St ____ Zip ____ Phone

Current Address _____ Street ____ City ____ St ____ Zip ____ Phone

Date of Birth __4/6/67?__ Ht. __6.5__ Wt. __225__ Bats __R__ Throws __R__ PHASE __R__ DATE ELIGIBLE __JUNE 85__

Game Date(s) __APR. 9-85__ Games __1__ Innings __7__ Graduation __JUNE 85__

No.	RATING KEY	M.P.H.	NON-PITCHERS	Pres.	Fut.	PITCHERS	Pres.	Fut.	MAKEUP				
8	Outstanding	94-	Hitting Ability			Fast Ball	6	6					
7	Very Good	91-93	Power			Life of Fastball	5	6		Ex.	Good	Fair	Poor
6	Above Average	88-90	Running Speed			Curve	3	4	Habits	4	3	2	1
5	Average	85-87	Base Running			Control	4	5	Dedication	4	3	2	1
4	Below Average	82-84	Arm Strength			Change of pace	✓	✓	Agility	4	3	2	1
3	Well Below Ave.	79-81	Arm Accuracy			Slider	✓	✓	Aptitude	4	3	2	1
2	Poor	0-78	Fielding			Other	✓	✓	Phys. Mat.	4	3	2	1
			Range			Poise	5	5	Emot. Mat.	4	3	2	1

USE ONE GRADE	Hitting: (✓)	Running						Baseball Inst.	4	3	2	1
Grade On	Pull ....3 ____	Time To	Arm Action	EX 4	GOOD 3	FAIR 2	POOR 1	Aggressive- ness	4	3	2	1
Major League	St. Away ....2 ____	1st Base		3/4	OH	SIDE	OTHER					
Standard	Opp. Field..1 ____		Delivery	8	3	2	1	OVERALL	4	3	2	1
			Gun Reading __86__ to __88__ MPH									

Physical Description (Injuries, Glasses, etc.) BIG - COULD HAVE WEIGHT PROBLEM THRU HIP AREA COULD WEIGH 215 + HAVE MORE FLEXIBILITY. BUILT LIKE NOLAN RYAN.

Abilities SIZE, COORDINATION + BODY CONTROL GOOD FOR BIG PITCHES. SHOWS M.L. FB - MOVEMENT GOOD AT TIMES. TAILS + RIDES. CLOCKED EARLIER AT 90 MPH. DID NOT SEE IN THIS OUTING. BASIC DELIVERY FROM FULL WINDUP - GOOD - FINISHES PROPERLY

Weaknesses MECHANICS ON CURVE NEED HELP. ARM MAY BE TIRED. DROPPED BELOW 3/4 ON FB. DELIVERY OFTEN. DID SLING BALL! WAS NOT FREE AT TIMES. FROM STRETCH - NO LEG ACTION. ALL ARM + VELOCITY WENT TO 84-85. ARM ACTION NOT AS FREE AS YOU WOULD LIKE TO SEE.

Signability: Ex._____ Good_____ Fair __✓__ Poor_____ Worth: $ __35,000__

MAY NOT BE ABLE TO SIGN FOR ABOVE FIGURE. WANTS TO GO OUT + PLAY NOW. PARENTS + BOY WILL DECIDE.

Makeup Evaluation and Player Summation HAS THE MAKING OF A GOOD PITCHER WITH SOME COACHING. PLENTY OF MAJOR SCHOOLS ARE AFTER HIM. VISITED OKLA.

MARK GUBICZA

*W*hen Mark Gubicza pitched for William Penn Charter High School in Philadelphia, he was very impressive. At 6'6" and 210 pounds at eighteen years of age, he resembled a Sequoia on the mound, and the ball looked like a nonpareil shot out of a bazooka coming at the plate. He was selected by the Royals in the second round of the 1981 draft. The pitcher selected in the next round by the Royals is his current teammate David Cone, who pitched at Rockhurst High in the Royals' backyard in Kansas City.

When reading early reports on major leaguers, you try to find an observation that later proves to be a key to the player's performance. In Gubicza's case, the weakness that the scout saw—"tries to overthrow at times"—may help explain why Mark has not become the pitcher he might have been. In 1982, after a brilliant rookie season with the Gulf Coast Royals, where he had an 8–1 won–loss record, he was placed on the disabled list with a bad arm. He recovered and was brought up to Kansas City in 1984. When the Royals were in the 1985 AL championship playoffs, Toronto needed one more win to clinch the title. Gubicza was called on to be the stopper. He beat the Jays, and Kansas City went on to take the championship four games to three. That year and the following season Gubicza was on the AL All-Star teams. But his arm trouble recurred in 1990 when, after an early 4–7 start, he went on the DL for the rest of the season and underwent rotator cuff surgery. He returned in 1991 and has not had a winning season since.

On May 1, 1994, Gubicza won his first game as a starter in two years and was 7–9 with a 4.50 ERA when the season folded in August 1994.

KANSAS CITY ROYALS
FREE AGENT REPORT

Overall future potential __65__   Report No. _1_

PLAYER ___GUBICZA___ ___MARK___ ___STEVEN___   Position _RHP_
         (Last name)   (First name)   (Middle name)

Current Address ___593 MONASTERY AVE.___ ___PHILA___ ___PA___ ___19128___
                                           (City)   (State)   (Zip Code)

Telephone _215_ _483- 5671_ Date of Birth _8/14/62_ Ht. _6 6_ Wt. _210_ Bats _R_ Throws _R_
    (Area Code)

Permanent address (if different from above) ___SAME___

Team Name _PENN CARTER H.S._ City _PHILA_   State _PA_

Scout ___TOM FERRICK___ Date _4/22/81_ Race _W_ Games _1_ Innings _7_

RATING KEY	NON-PITCHERS	Pres.	Fut.	PITCHERS	Pres.	Fut.	USE WORD DESCRIPTION
8–Outstanding	Hitting Ability	*		Fast Ball	* 5	6	Habits _Good_
7–Very Good	Power	*		Curve	* —	—	Dedication _Good_
6–Above Average	Running Speed	*		Control	4	5	Agility _U Good_
5–Average	Base Running			Change of Pace	4	5	Aptitude _Good_
4–Below Average	Arm Strength	*		Slider	* 4	6	Phys. Maturity _U Good_
3–Well Below Average	Arm Accuracy			Knuckle Ball			Emot. Maturity _Good_
2–Poor	Fielding	*		Other	*		Married _NO_
	Range			Poise	5	5	
Use One Grade	Baseball Instinct			Baseball Instinct	5	5	Date Eligible
Grade On Major	Aggressiveness			Aggressiveness	5	6	_JUNE 81_
League Standards	Pull Str. Away		Opp. Field	Arm Action _Good_			Phase
Not Amateur	___ ___		___	Delivery _Good_			_REG_

Physical Description (Injuries, Glasses, etc.)   GRADUATION ___6/81___
GOOD ATHLETIC BODY- WELL PROPORTIONED - BASKETBALL PLAYER.
STRONG + AGGRESSIVE ON MOUND.

Abilities FINE BODY COORDINATION. BODY CONTROL + MECHANICS ARE ALL GOOD
FOR BIG PITCHER. FB CONSISTENTLY 5 ML - SINKS + TAILS. THROWS
HEAVY BALL. SOME FAST BALLS CLOSE TO 6 ML. QUICK OFF MOUND FIELDING.
GOOD MOVE TO 1B. CURVE MORE LIKE BIG SLIDER. BREAKS SHARPLY
DOWN. COMMAND OF PITCHES GOOD FOR H.S. PITCHER.

Weaknesses TENDS TO OVERTHROW AT TIMES.

Summation and Signability GOOD ML POTENTIAL. HAS COLLEGE OFFERS. GOOD ATHLETE.
FATHER PLAYED IN W. SOX ORG EARLY 50'S. WORKS POST OFFICE. WOULD BE
HAPPY TO HAVE AS OUR NO. 1 PICK. SHOULD GO IN TOP 10 IN COUNTRY.
I LIKE HIM VERY MUCH. COMPETES WELL. WILL SIGN IF MONEY IS ACCEPTABLE.

DON GULLETT

When you look at Don Gullett's major league record, you're struck by the heights he attained and from which he so suddenly fell. And if you don't know why a pitcher with a 14–4 record one year quit the next season, then take a look at the following scouting report. It may give you a clue.

When Tom Ferrick saw Gullett, he was an eighteen-year-old Kentucky high school pitcher. Ferrick believed he had found a future major leaguer, no doubt about it. And Tom was right. He urged the Royals to pick him in the first round of the 1969 draft. But it was to prove to be a very disappointing draft for Kansas City.

The Royals had the twenty-third pick and, before their turn came, Cincinnati chose Gullett. Unfortunately for Kansas City, of their first five picks in that draft, only two players even made it to the majors, and they played a total of nine big league games.

Gullett went on to become an outstanding pitcher for the Reds, posting the best NL won–loss average in 1971, .727 with a 16–6 record. In 1975 he again was tops in the NL with .789 in a 15–4 year. He had speed and control and in his nine seasons had a 3.11 ERA while striking out an average of six men per game and walking only three.

In 1977 Gullett signed as a free agent with the Yankees, who gave him a handsome five-year contract. He started meteorically for New York in 1977 with a 14–4 record, but the following year the arm trouble that had plagued him all during his career became severe, and it didn't respond to treatment. In 1978, after winning only four games, Gullett left baseball, doubling Yankees' owner George Steinbrenner's suffering. Not only did Gullett fail to give George the pitching he needed, but George had to pay Gullett for the three remaining years on his contract while the ex-Yankee sat in his old Kentucky home.

The early report on Gullett is an example of a scout's astuteness and attention to detail. As far back as when Gullett was in high school, Ferrick noted that he threw "across his body." It didn't seem a problem at the time, but many believe that years of using such an unorthodox motion damaged Gullett's arm progressively and finally cut short a brilliant career.

KANSAS CITY ROYALS
FREE AGENT
PROSPECT REPORT

May 16, 1969

WHAT TYPE OF PROSPECT?
(EXCELLENT) (Definite Prospect) ✔
GOOD (Prospect) _____
FAIR (Has Chance) _____

PLAYER INFORMATION   PLEASE PRINT OR TYPE   Position *LHP*

NAME _Gullet_ (Last)   _Donald_ (First)   _Edward_ (Middle)   Hgt _6'1_ Wgt _190_   Bats _R_ Throws _L_

Complete Address _____
Date of Birth _____   Telephone _____
Parent's Name _____   Telephone _____
Parent's Address _____
Family Physician _____   Telephone _____
Complete Address _____
Name of High School _McKell HS South Shore Ken_   Graduation Date _____
Name of College _____   Graduation Date _____
Was player ever a member of an American Legion Team? _____
Has player ever signed a professional baseball contract? _____
If so, when? _____ With what club? _____   Is he now a Free Agent? _Yes_
Military Status: _____   Discharge Date: _____
Has player ever been selected in the Free Agent Draft? _No_   By what club(s) _____
Player recommended by _____   Address _____

SCOUT REPORT   PLEASE PRINT OR TYPE
Observation Period _May 16, 1969_ Games _1_   Workouts _____
ARM: Strength _____   Accuracy _____
FIELDING: Range _____   Hands _____   Body Control _____
HITTING: Ability _____   Power _____
RUNNING: Speed _____   Base Running Ability _____

PITCHER: Fast Ball _2_ Curve _3+2_ Change _none_ Control _3_

DESCRIPTIVE REMARKS: good velocity ML at Prime good for HS pitcher

Aptitude: _____ Other Pitch: _____   Type of Delivery: _____   Poise: _good_
Aggressiveness: _good_   Habits: _____
Does this player have health problems?: _No_
Physical Description (Build, size, agility, etc.) _Sturdy, strong body with proportional good sturdy legs_
In what class of Pro Ball can he start? _Rookie_
List other Clubs that scouted player (Give Scout's name) _All clubs_

Describe this player in detail, giving any information you feel is important:
Has good potential Definite ML prospect

REPORTED BY: _____
SCOUT
(Grade as follows: 1 - Excellent; 2 - Good; 3 - Average; 4 - Poor)
K. C. 8   USE OTHER SIDE FOR ADDITIONAL INFORMATION

59

Donald Gullet LHP 6:01 190"

Good poise for youngster. Delivery between 3/4 & overhand. Good velocity on FB. Action good when down, mainly straight when up. Curve good ML at times. Showed best curve of any young pitcher I have seen all year.

Finishes delivery with stiff right leg. Pitches straight up & finishes nearly same way. Good coordination rhythm & body cntrl. Throws slightly across body but not enough to hinder fluid delivery.

Good sturdy, strong body with good legs. Aggressive & poised on mound. Agile fielding position.

I rate him excellent ML prospect. Should go in ML draft easily.

PETE HARNISCH

*N*ineteen ninety-four was supposed to be a big year for Pete Harnisch. The former Fordham University star had re-signed with the Astros for an arbitrated $3.2 million contract, and the world was his oyster. No one could know that two months into the season, Harnisch would be facing a career-ending injury. After being pounded for a 7.15 ERA in April and May, Harnisch was put on the DL with a torn tendon in his right shoulder. He returned in July, but things didn't get much better. Harnisch ended the aborted 1994 season with an 8–5 mark and a 5.40 ERA. The Astros could be stuck with $3.2 million worth of *caveat emptor*, which even in Latin is a hell of a lot of caveat.

Harnisch was drafted in 1987 by the Orioles as their supplemental first choice, a choice given to Baltimore as compensation for Cleveland's signing of free agent Rick Dempsey. Harnisch started fast at Bluefield in the Appalachian League, posting a 3–1 record with a 2.56 ERA before moving up to Hagerstown and the next season to Charlotte and Rochester. With four teams in the minors, Harnisch never had higher than a 2.58 ERA. Joining the Orioles in late '88, he struggled in '89 and was sent back to Rochester. In 1990 Harnisch posted an 11–11 record for the Orioles with an indifferent 4.34 ERA. Baltimore traded him to Houston before the 1991 season, and with the Astros he started to fulfill his potential. That year he led the team in wins with twelve, had the Astros' best ERA (2.70), most strikeouts (172), and complete games (4), and was voted to the '91 All-Star team.

After a disappointing '92 season, Harnisch got hot in '93. He won sixteen games with a 2.98 ERA and led the league in shutouts with four. He averaged over 7.6 strikeouts per game and pitched two one-hitters. It couldn't have happened at a better time for Harnisch. The following year he was up for arbitration, and Harnisch had Houston by the horse hairs. How will it all turn out, considering Harnisch's alarming injury? Time will tell—in New York, as the Mets picked up Harnisch in the '94 post-season.

KANSAS CITY ROYALS
FREE AGENT REPORT

OFFICE USE
Report No. _____
Player No. _____

Overall Future Potential ___5 6___

Nat'l. Double Check   Yes __✓__ No_____

Scout's Report # ___1___   Scout ___FERRICK___

PLAYER ___HARNISCA   PETER   S.___ Pos. ___RHP___ Date __4/20/87__
    Last Name   First Name   Middle Initial

School or Team ___FORDHAM UNIV___ City and State ___NYC, NY___

Permanent Address _____ Street   City   St   Zip   Phone

Current Address _____ Street   City   St   Zip   Phone

Date of Birth _9/23/66_ Ht. _6_ Wt. _185_ Bats _R_ Throws _R_ DATE ELIGIBLE _JUNE '87_ PHASE _R_

Game Date(s) _APR. 20 '87_ Games _1_ Innings _7_ Graduation _JUNE '88_

No.	RATING KEY	M.P.H.	NON-PITCHERS	Pres.	Fut.	PITCHERS	Pres.	Fut.	MAKEUP
8—Outstanding	94-		Hitting Ability			Fast Ball	5	5	
7—Very Good	91-93		Power			Life of Fastball	4	4	
6—Above Average	88-90		Running Speed			Curve	2	3	
5—Average	85-87		Base Running			Control	4	5	
4—Below Average	82-84		Arm Strength			Change of Pace	—	—	
3—Well Below Ave.	79-81		Arm Accuracy			Slider	3	4	
2—Poor	0-78		Fielding			Other SPLIT	3	4	
			Range			Poise	5	5	

MAKEUP	Ex.	Good	Fair	Poor
Habits	✓	3	2	1
Dedication	4	3✓	2	1
Agility	✓	3	2	1
Aptitude	4	3✓	2	1
Phys. Mat.	4	3✓	2	1
Emot. Mat.	4	3✓	2	1
Baseball Inst.	4	3✓	2	1
Aggressive-ness	4	3✓	2	1
OVERALL	4	3✓	2	1

USE ONE GRADE
Grade On
Major League
Standard

Hitting: (√)
Pull ....3_____
St. Away ....2_____
Opp. Field .. 1_____

Running
Time To
1st Base

Arm Action	EX	GOOD	FAIR	POOR
	4	3✓	2	1

Delivery	3/4	OH	SIDE	OTHER
	4✓	3	2	1

Gun Reading __85__ to __87__ MPH

Physical Description (Injuries, Glasses, etc.) NO GLASSES- NO KNOWN INSURIES. GOOD STRONG ATHLETIC BODY. PHYSICALLY MATURED.

Abilities ARM STRENGTH. GOOD BODY + SIZE. AGILE & QUICK ON MOUND. GOOD MOVE TO 1B. COMPETITIVE + GOOD MAKEUP. ML VELOCITY ON F.B. - 85-87. FLUID DELIVERY. COORDINATION + ROTATION ARE GOOD.

Weaknesses FB. STRAIGHT + HITTABLE. NEEDS MOVEMENT. SLIDER - NO DRIVE TO IT. CURVE NOT GOOD. SPLIT FINGER MIGHT HELP BUT NOT VERY SOON. DELIVERY EASY TO FOLLOW. BREAKING BALL NEEDS HELP AS DOES FB FOR MOVEMENT

Signability: Ex._____ Good_____ Fair _✓_ Poor_____ Worth: $ _20-25,000_
WANTS TO GO OUT NOW.

Makeup Evaluation and Player Summation GOOD MAKEUP + WORK HABITS. HAS POTENTIAL WILL NEED SOME PRO HELP. ARM + MAKEUP ARE HIS TWO PLUSES RIGHT NOW.

TEDDY HIGUERA

TED HIGUERA

*H*iguera must have thought he would never get out of his native Mexico. He spent five years playing for Ciudad Juarez in the Mexican League. He had a good year in 1981 with sixteen wins, and yet the phone hadn't rung with a single offer from a big-league club. Then in 1983 he hit his stride and his fastball was dancing. Higuera posted a Mexican League–leading seventeen wins, eighteen complete games and registered 165 strikeouts with a dandy 2.03 ERA. The phone rang.

He went to El Paso where he led the Texas League with a tidy 2.60 ERA. At the tail end of the season, Higuera's contract was bought by Vancouver, the Pacific Coast affiliate of the Milwaukee Brewers. He was one step away from the majors. In 1985 he started the season with the parent Brewers and enjoyed a tremendous rookie season. Higuera led the Brewers with his fifteen wins and 212 innings pitched and registered the most strikeouts, 207, on the Milwaukee staff. His was the fourth highest winning percentage in the AL. In 1986 Higuera was even better, with twenty victories and 240 strikeouts and for the next two years was among the league leaders in won-loss percentage, strikeouts, complete games, and ERA.

When fate wants to deal someone a bad blow, it starts looking at the top and works its way down. In 1989 it started with Ted Higuera. He went on the disabled list for the first time but, unfortunately, not the last. He has been on the DL no less than six times. He has never recovered his earlier promise and now, at age thirty-six, it seems he never will. However, when you count Higuera out, you'll have a tough time convincing the Kansas City Royals. He has beaten them eight times against only one defeat. Higuera's career seemingly consists of a long wait, a four-year burst of glory, and then a startlingly rapid decline.

MILWAUKEE BREWERS
FREE AGENT REPORT

Overall future potential __55__   Report No. __1__

PLAYER ___Higuera___   ___Teodoro___   ___V___   Position __L H P__
          Last name   First name   Middle name

Current Address _____
                                   City   State   Zip Code

Telephone _____ Date of Birth _____ Ht. _5'10_"Wt. _170_ Bats _L_ Throws _L_
        (Area Code)

Permanent address (if different from above) _____

Team Name ___Juarez___   City ___Juarez___   State ___Mexico___

Scout _____ Date _8/29/83_ Race ___M___ Games ___1___ Innings _8 2/3_

RATING KEY	NON-PITCHERS	Power Freq.	Pres.	Fut.	PITCHERS	Move-ment	Pres.	Fut.	USE WORD DESCRIPTION
8—Outstanding	Hitting Ability *				Fast Ball *	5	6	6	Habits _____
7—Very Good	Power *				Curve *		5	5	Dedication _____
6—Above Average	Running Speed *				Control		5	5	Agility ___Good___
5—Average	Base Running				Change of Pace		0	0	Aptitude _____
4—Below Average	Arm Strength *				Slider *		0	0	Phys. Maturity ___Good___
3—Well Below Average	Arm Accuracy				Knuckle Ball		0	0	Emot. Maturity_____
2—Poor	Fielding *				Other *		0	0	Married _____
	Range				Poise		5	5	
Use One Grade	Baseball Instinct				Baseball Instinct		6	6	Date Eligible
Grade On Major	Aggressiveness				Aggressiveness		6	6	
League Standards	Pull Str. Away	Opp. Field			Arm Action ___Good___				Phase
Not Amateur	_____ _____	_____			Delivery ___Good–H 3/4___				

Physical Description (Injuries, Glasses, etc.)   GRADUATION _____
    Medium solid build. Has very good shoulders. Wiry strong type.

Abilities   Fastball has average movement, runs into LHH. Fastball ranged from 85 to 90, threw only a couple 84, and threw a couple 90. Most of the time his FB was 87 & 88. His curve ball has good rotation and break. His control was at least average and maybe better. His curveball was 71 to 74. Very agg on mound, challenges hitters with his FB most of time. He has quick arm action. Fielded his position well.

Weaknesses Did not throw but two pitches all night, FB and CB, Threw only one change. Has confidence in his FB. Needs to throw more change ups. He also has a slider which he did not use all night. His manager Guerrero who I played against when I managed in Mexico, said he has four pitches, FB, CB, Slider, and a Straight Ch that has a little screwball action, but he needs work on it.

Summation and Signability   Worth _$35,000_____

    Higuera was very impress with aggressiveness and his determination to get the players out. He has two ML pitches at this time FB and CB. His control also is average ML. His abilities are better than any LHP that we have in our organization at present time. All though he is a starter, I think that he could possibly become a short reliefer. I think we should try and get him.

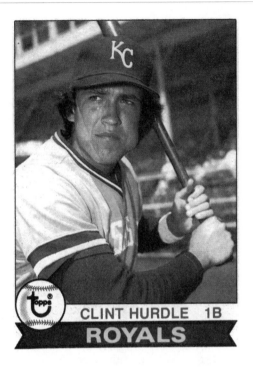

CLINT HURDLE 1B
ROYALS

CLINT HURDLE

W hat do scouts do in the off-season? Some use the down time to
try to figure out why the prospect who looked so great failed
to live up to their expectations. Being wrong is hard for most of our
species to admit, and we can find deviously creative ways of shifting
the burden of blame onto other people. If not them, then blame it on
exigencies that are beyond our control. Kismet gone cockeyed. Mis-
takes can be interred in our psyches in unmarked graves to be exhumed,
if ever, by those ghouls of the unconscious, the analysts.

But a scout makes a judgment and a commitment and he puts it
down on paper. When he's wide of the mark, his error can become an
open wound that will continue to fester. Take a youngster like the not-
yet-eighteen-year-old Clint Hurdle in 1975. He was a surefire prospect, as his scouting report indicates.

The first round of the June 1975 major league draft was not loaded with a huge cargo of talent. Of all the players selected first, none became significant major leaguers. The best recognized name is journeyman catcher Rick Cerone, who put in time with eight clubs. However, some prospects who were overlooked in the first round were real sleepers: relief pitcher Lee Smith, whose lifetime ERA is under 3.00; third baseman Carney Lansford who was AL Batting Champion in 1981 with a .336 BA; second baseman Lou Whitaker, who has been a regular for the Tigers ever since 1978; and Andre Dawson, who has starred for the Expos, Cubs, and Red Sox. So much for hindsight.

But Clint Hurdle was the kid to get in '75, and the Royals were delighted to grab him. Then it happened. Or more aptly, then it didn't happen. *Sports Illustrated* welcomed him into the majors with his picture on its front cover in 1978. Clint had no way of knowing that this would be the highlight of his career.

"In Kansas City," Tom Ferrick told me, "Clint started hanging around with the wrong people. His skill started to diminish, and when he went to Venezuela and played in the off-season, he picked up more bad habits." Hurdle played at Kansas City off and on until 1981, during which time he had one good season. In 1980 Clint hit .294. He went five for twelve in that year's World Series against the victorious Phillies. By 1987, at the age of 30, and after trying unsuccessfully to make it as an outfielder, first and third baseman, and catcher, Clint called it quits as a player.

There's an irony about his home run potential. His report indicates that Clint could hit twenty-five or thirty homers per season. He actually did hit thirty-two homers, but it was the total for his entire career. Ferrick says that story has a happy ending. "He had a second chance," says Ferrick, "and wound up managing a Triple A club for the Mets. Now he's straightened out his life. He's a wonderful young man."

KANSAS CITY ROYALS
FREE AGENT REPORT

A CAN'T MISS THAT MISSED

Overall future potential __70__

Report No. __1__

PLAYER __HURDLE__ (Last name) __CLINT__ (First name) ____ (Middle name) Position __C.F.__

Current Address _____ (City) ____ (State) ____ (Zip Code)

Telephone ____ (Area Code) ____ Date of Birth __6__ Ht. __6:3__ Wt. __175__ Bats __L__ Throws __R__

Permanent address (If different from above) _____

Team Name __MERRITT ISL. H.S.__ City __MERRITT ISLAND__ State __FLA__

Scout __TOM FERRICK__ Date __3/31/75__ Race __W__ Games __1__ Innings __7__

RATING KEY	NON-PITCHERS	Pres.	Fut.	PITCHERS	Pres.	Fut.	USE WORD DESCRIPTION
8–Outstanding	Hitting Ability	5	7	Fast Ball			Habits __Good__
7–Very Good	Power	6	7	Curve			Dedication __V Good__
6–Above Average	Running Speed	43	43	Control			Agility __Good__
5–Average	Base Running	4	5	Change of Pace			Aptitude __Good__
4–Below Average	Arm Strength	5	5	Slider			Phys. Maturity __Good__
3–Well Below Average	Arm Accuracy	5	5	Knuckle Ball			Emot. Maturity __Good__
2–Poor	Fielding	5	6	Other			Married __No__
	Range	5	5	Poise			
Use One Grade	Baseball Instinct	6	7	Baseball Instinct			Date Eligible
Grade On Major	Aggressiveness	6	7	Aggressiveness			
League Standards	Pull ✓ Str. Away Opp. Field			Arm Action _____			Phase
Not Amateur	____ ____ ____			Delivery _____			__REGULAR__

Physical Description (Injuries, Glasses, etc.)

GOOD ATHLETIC BODY. RANGY + STRONG

Abilities ARM AVERAGE. BODY CONTROL + AGILITY GOOD. CONDITION
GOOD. GOOD BAT SPEED + HAS A LIVE BAT. ABOVE AVERAGE P5550
BAT MECHANICS GOOD FOR YOUNG HITTER RUNS 4.3. HANDS GOOD.
COULD PLAY R.F. + L.F. + CF. (ADEQUATELY)

Weaknesses SHORT ARMS HIS THROWS OCCASIONALLY (FB. QUARTER BACK
+ HAS DEVELOPED QUICK - SHORT ARM RELEASE) BUT SHOWED IN CF
THROWS THAT HE COULD ADJUST.

Summation and Signability SHOULD BE GOOD EVERYDAY M.L. O.F. WITH
25 OR 30 HR. POWER. SHOULD BE SHADE BETTER THAN AVERAGE
DEFENSIVE PLAYER. COMPETITIVE. GOOD MA + LIKES TO PLAY.
GOING TO COST $55,000 TO 50,000. BUT IS WORTH IT TO KEEP IN
BASEBALL

JIMMY KEY

W hen Key was a senior at Butler High School in Huntsville, Alabama, he was picked number ten by the White Sox in the 1979 draft. Jimmy felt he was better than that and decided to go to Clemson instead. Three years later, as a college junior, he was drafted by the Blue Jays in the third round. Even though Tom Ferrick noted on his report that he "missed on evaluation" of Key in the one game he saw him work, Ferrick was correct when he suggested that Key would have to be "a finesse type pitcher." Finesse is Key's bread and butter. He likes to get ahead of the batter and has the remarkable ability of getting the first strike. Since hitters know that the first pitch will be over the plate, they try to sit on it. But Key mixes up his pitches, hits the corners, and keeps the ball low. This adroitness has kept hitters off balance and off the bases for eleven years.

When Key joined the Yankees as a free agent in 1993 after nine years with Toronto, he received the eighth highest salary in baseball, $5.2 million per year. That figures out to $22,183.72 for every inning he pitched in 1993. But thanks to his 18–6 mark and a 3.00 ERA, the Yankees aren't complaining. And seemingly neither are the fans, who chip in for Key's salary by paying $3.75 for a one-buck hot dog and the same for a fifty-cent Coke while enjoying the view at Yankee Stadium.

When Key was with Toronto he had an overall 116–81 won-loss record, and his 2.76 ERA in 1987 was the best in the AL. In the 1992 World Series against the Braves, Key shut out Atlanta for eight innings for the win and came back in the sixth game for his second series victory to take the World Championship outside the United States for the first time in history. In the abbreviated 1994 season, Key led the AL in wins with a 17–4 record. In one ten-week stretch he won eleven straight games.

It's interesting to note that his 1982 report indicates that Key was a good hitter. We don't know if this still holds true since Jimmy has spent his career in the AL, where he has never come to bat because of the designated hitter.

KANSAS CITY ROYALS

FREE AGENT REPORT *MISSED ON EVALUATION*

Overall future potential __46__

PLAYER __KEY__ __JAMES__ __EDWARD__ Position __LHP__ Report No. __1__
Last name / First name / Middle name

Current Address _____

Telephone _____ Date of Birth __4/22/61__ Ht. __6-1__ Wt. __181__ Bats __R__ Throws __L__
(Area Code)   City   State   Zip Code

Permanent address (if different from above) _____

Team Name __CLEMSON UNIV.__ City __CLEMSON__ State __S.C.__

Scout __TOM FERRICK__ Date __4/22/82__ Race __W__ Games __1__ Innings __7__

RATING KEY	NON-PITCHERS		Pres.	Fut.	PITCHERS		Pres.	Fut.	USE WORD DESCRIPTION
8–Outstanding	Hitting Ability	*			Fast Ball	*	4	4	Habits _____
7–Very Good	Power	*			Curve	*	4	5	Dedication _____
6–Above Average	Running Speed	*			Control		4	5	Agility __GOOD__
5–Average	Base Running				Change of Pace		5	6	Aptitude _____
4–Below Average	Arm Strength	*			Slider	*	4	4	Phys. Maturity _____
3–Well Below Average	Arm Accuracy				Knuckle Ball		–	–	Emot. Maturity _____
2–Poor	Fielding	*			Other	*			Married __NO__
	Range				Poise		5	5	
Use One Grade	Baseball Instinct				Baseball Instinct		4	5	Date Eligible
Grade On Major	Aggressiveness				Aggressiveness		5	5	__JUNE 82__
League Standards	Pull Str. Away Opp. Field				Arm Action __FAIR__				Phase
Not Amateur	___ ___ ___				Delivery __FAIR__				__REG__

Physical Description (Injuries, Glasses, etc.) GRADUATION __JUNE 83__

TALL - RANGY GOOD BODY FOR ATHLETE

Abilities SIZE. SOME ARM STRENGTH. AGILE FIELDER.
SLO CHANGE 5-6 M.L. FAIR COMMAND, FB SLIGHT
TAILING ACTION AT TIMES. BETTER CONTROL ON CURVE
& SL CHANGE THAN FB. SWINGS BAT WELL FOR PITCHER,
PH (PINCH HITS) AT TIMES.

Weaknesses FB 4 ML. PITCHES AROUND IT. CURVE ROLLING TYPE.
NOT MUCH DRIVE ON IT. THROWS ACROSS BODY AT TIMES.
POOR MOVE TO 1B. HAS TROUBLE FINDING CORNER WITH FB.

Summation and Signability CAN'T SEE HIM GETTING ANY FASTER AT 21 YEARS OF AGE.
WILL HAVE TO BE FINESSE TYPE PITCHER. COMPETES FAIRLY WELL.
NEEDS HELP IN MOST PHASES OF PITCHING. HIS BAT MAY WIND UP
BEING HIS BIGGEST ASSET. POSITION ?

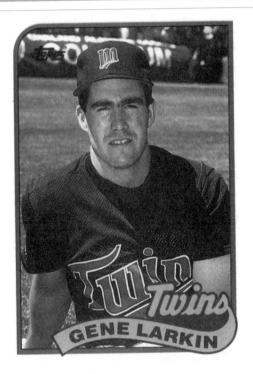

GENE LARKIN

*T*he report on Larkin indicates that he would never make the majors as a third baseman, the position he played the most in college. The idea of switching him to first base had a certain resonance to it. Now it's true that Columbia University is not a school that's known for contributing athletes to the pros—with one luminous exception: a first baseman named Lou Gehrig who played at Columbia in 1923. If only Larkin could follow in his illustrious predecessor's footsteps. . . .

Larkin was selected by Minnesota in the twentieth round of the 1984 draft after graduating from the Ivy League school. He was sent to Elizabeth in the Appalachian League, where he became a full-time first baseman and led the league in double plays while batting a solid .326. Promoted to Visalia of the California League in '85, Larkin led the league in RBIs with 106 and hit .305. With Orlando in '86 he posted a

.321 BA and the following year hit .302 at Portland before being called up to the Twins. In a little over three years in the minors, Larkin's BA was .312.

At Minnesota in 1987 he played in eighty-five games and saw action in the World Series when he pinch-hit a double as the Twins beat the Cardinals in seven games. The next season Larkin was Minnesota's designated hitter and batted .267. From '89 to '93 he was used as a utility man, pinch hitter, and DH. In the World Series of '91, Larkin pinch-hit four times and singled twice, including the winning hit in the seventh game, helping Minnesota to overcome the Braves four games to three.

Larkin never did become a second Lou Gehrig, but he did prove to be a valuable and versatile player. In his last year, 1993, he even played third base again. Apparently what goes around does come around.

MINNESOTA TWINS BASEBALL CLUB

PLAYER INFORMATION CARD

POSITION 3B – 1B

NAME LARKIN EUGENE THOMAS
(Last) (First) (Middle)
BATS S HGT. 6-3
THROWS R WGT. 195

ADDRESS 916 BELLMORE ROAD NO. BELLMORE 11710 NY
(Number) (Street) (City) (P.O. Zone) (State)

DATE OF BIRTH 10 24 1964 TELEPHONE 516-221-9127
(Month) (Day) (Year)

PARENT'S NAME EUGENE

NAME AND ADDRESS OF HIGH SCHOOL OR COLLEGE COLUMBIA UNIV NYC

DATE OF YOUR GRADUATION FROM HIGH SCHOOL OR COLLEGE 6 1984
(Month) (Day) (Year)

ARE YOU A MEMBER OF AN AMERICAN JUNIOR LEGION JUNIOR TEAM? —

HAVE YOU EVER SIGNED A PROFESSIONAL BASEBALL CONTRACT? —
(Where) (What Club)

ARE YOU NOW A FREE AGENT? — MILITARY STATUS STUDENT

PHYSICAL DESCRIPTION (BUILD, SIZE, AGILITY, ETC.) GOOD ALL THE WAY (OTHER SIDE)

HABITS

CLASSIFICATION IN WHICH SHOULD PLAY NEXT YEAR: A

PLAYER RECOMMENDED BY: HERB STEIN REPORT BY: Herb Stein DATE MAY 1984

SCOUT REPORT SECTION

CLUB & LEAGUE COLUMBIA UNIV
LENGTH OF OBSERVATION 3 GAMES
ARM 5-5 ACCURACY 5-6
FIELDING 5-5
HITTING 4— POWER 5-6
RUNNING SPEED 4 BASE RUNNING

PITCHER
SPEED
CURVE
CHANGE
CONTROL

APTITUDE OK REACTIONS OK
AGGRESSIVENESS OK
DEFINITE PROSPECT?
HAS CHANCE? ✓
OTHER REMARKS

"THIS IS A BIG STRONG BOY. HE CAN HIT WITH POWER. VERY AGGRESIVE. I SUGGEST HE FORGET PLAYING 3RD BASE AND BREAK IN AS FIRST BASE MEN. HE CAN FIELD, HAS GOOD ARM, BUT HAS POOR THROW, OVER HAND ALL THE TIME. LOSES TIME GETTING RID OF BALL AT 3RD B. HE'S WORTH A SHOT. NEGLIGIBLE BONUS. WANTS TO PLAY."

GREG MADDUX

W hen Greg Maddux graduated from Valley High in Las Vegas, he didn't want to spend three more years in college before trying his luck in pro ball. His older brother Mike had gone to college before he signed with the Philadelphia Phillies in 1982 and then spent ten years going up and down in the minors. Greg was looking for faster answers about his baseball career. Even though the Mets were high on Maddux, they were even higher on Shawn Abner, a "can't miss" outfield prospect, and Lorenzo Sisney, a catcher from California. The following are reports on Maddux from the Mets and the Major League Scouting Bureau.

The Mets passed on Maddux twice and the Cubs grabbed him. Shawn Abner went on to a short, disappointing career, and Lorenzo Sisney never made it to the majors.

Maddux was in the minors less than three years when he joined the Cubs in 1986, just after his twentieth birthday. With the Cubs over the next seven years Maddux became one of the premier pitchers in the National League. In 1989, his second full year at Chicago, Maddux led his team to the NL East Championship with nineteen wins. In 1992 his twenty wins tied him for the league lead, and he won the Cy Young Award. In 1993 Maddux joined the Braves as a free agent and won it again. He had a 20–10 season and was best in the NL with a stingy 2.36 ERA.

With Atlanta he was teamed up with Steve Avery, John Smoltz, and Tom Glavine to give the Braves the best pitching staff in the major leagues and they won the '93 NL West Championship. Maddux is a workhorse and has averaged over thirty starts in his eight-year career. Three times Maddux has led the NL in innings pitched. In 1994 he had the best ERA in the majors, 1.56, with a 16–6 record. A word of warning: In the highly unlikely event that you ever come to bat against Greg Maddux, don't dig in too hard. He's also led the NL in hit batsmen.

MAJOR LEAGUE SCOUTING BUREAU

FREE AGENT REPORT

Overall future potential __55.8__   Report No. __1__

PLAYER __MADDUX__ (Last name)   __GREGORY__ (First name)   __ALAN__ (Middle name)   Position __RHP__

Current Address _____

City _____ State _____ Zip Code

Telephone __702-456-0154__ (Area Code)   Date of Birth _____ Ht. ____ Wt. ____ Bats __R__ Throws __R__

Permanent address (If different from above) __Same__

Team Name __VALLEY H.S.__   City __LAS VEGAS__   State __Nev.__

Scout __D. BOGARD__   Date __04-13-84__   Games __1__ Innings __7__

RATING KEY	NON-PITCHERS		Pres.	Fut.	PITCHERS	Pres.	Fut.	USE WORD DESCRIPTION	
8–Outstanding	Hitting Ability	*			Fast Ball ✓	*	5	6	Habits _good_
7–Very Good	Power	*			Curve	*	4	5	Dedication _good_
6–Above Average	Running Speed	*			Control		4	5	Agility _good_
5–Average	Base Running				Change of Pace		0	0	Aptitude _good_
4–Below Average	Arm Strength	*			Slider	*	0	0	Phys. Maturity _good_
3–Well Below Average	Arm Accuracy				Knuckle Ball		0	0	Emot. Maturity _good_
2–Poor	Fielding	*			Other	*	0	0	
	Range				Poise		4	5	
USE ONE GRADE	Baseball Instinct				Baseball Instinct		4	5	Date Eligible
Grade On Major	Aggressiveness				Aggressiveness		5	5	_06-84_
League Standards	Pull		Str. Away		_good_	Arm Action			Phase
Not Amateur					_fair_	Delivery			_Reg_

Physical Description (Injuries, Glasses, etc.)   GRADUATION __06-84__

AVE. HT. SLENDER, WIREY BUILD, ROOM TO FILL OUT.

Abilities

LOOSE ARM. AVE. VEL. ON SINKING FB, AB. AVE. ON OCC.
FAIR ROT. ON 3/4 CB. FAIR CONTROL. AGG. GOOD COMPETITOR.

Weaknesses

LONG STRIDE, LANDS ON STIFF FRONT LEG, TOUGH TIME
GETTING OVER IT. DOESN'T ALWAYS GET ON TOP OF CURVEBALL.

Summation and Signability   Worth _____

DOUBT IF HE'LL BE OVERPOWERING TYPE, BUT SHOULD THROW A
LOT OF GROUND BALLS. POT. TO BE FRONT LINE PITCHER.

NEW YORK METS

OFP # 60

First Report ☐
Supplemental ☒

FREE AGENT PLAYER REPORT

Date of Last Report

Player: MADDUX (LAST NAME) GREG (FIRST NAME) (MIDDLE NAME)   Nickname

Home Address _____ Street _____ City _____ State ____ Zip Code   Home Phone ( ) _____ Area Code

School Address _____ Street _____ City _____ State ____ Zip Code   School Phone ( ) _____ Area Code

Position: RHP   Bats R   Throws R   Hgt. 6-1   Wgt. 160   D.O.B. _____

Team Name: VALLEY H.S.   City: LAS VEGAS   State: NEV

Date Eligible: 6 MONTH 84 YEAR   Regular ☒   Secondary ☐   Grad. Date 6/84

Total Games Seen to Date: 1   Total Innings Pitched 7   DATE LAST GAME SEEN 3/23/84

RATING KEY	POSITION PLAYERS	Pres.	Fut.	PITCHERS	Pres.	Fut.	NON-PHYSICAL QUALITIES
8–Outstanding	Hitting Ability			Fast Ball Vel.	5	6	Aggressiveness
7–Very Good	Raw Power			Fast Ball Mvmt.	4	6	Drive
6–Above Average	Power Frequency			Curve Ball	4	6	Self-Confidence
5–Average	Running Speed			Slider	0	0	Mental Toughness
4–Below Average	Base Running			Change-Up	4	6	Pressure Player
3–Weak	Arm Strength			Other	0	0	Courage
2–Poor	Arm Accuracy			Overall Control	4	6	Dedication
	Fielding			Command	4	6	Coachability
Use Major League	Range			Poise	4	5	Work Habits
Grading Standards.	B. B. Instinct			B. B. Instinct	5	6	Off Field Habits
Do Not Use Plusses	(TYPE OF HITTER)			DELIVERY			OVERALL MAKEUP GRADE
or Minuses.	Pwr ____ Linedrive ____ Slap ____			OH __ H 3/4 X L 3/4 __ SA __ UH __			

PHYSICAL DESCRIPTION & INJURIES: Glasses ☐   Contacts ☐   Married: ☐ Yes ☐ No
ON SLIM SIDE   SHOULD FILL OUT

STRENGTHS: GOOD LIVE ARM - Gd DEL. THROWS WITH VERY LITTLE EFFORT
F.B. HAS AUG OR BETTER VEL. 84-89. CURVE IS SHARP 74-76 CHANGE
SHOWS PROMISE. GOOD CONTROL FOR H.S. PITCHER.

WEAKNESSES: DROPS ARM AT TIMES. F.B. IS STRAIGHT WHEN UP.
SHOULD USE CHANGE MORE.

OVERALL SUMMATION: CAN REALLY PROJECT THIS BOY. HE SHOULD FILL OUT
AND GET STRONGER. HE THROWS WITH EASE AND SHOULD HAVE
GOOD CONTROL

SIGNABILITY DATA: Asking for $ _____   Actual Worth 50,000   Agent Involved   Yes ☐   No ☐

START AT WHAT LEVEL: _____

PROSPECT CATEGORY: Excellent ☐   Good ☒   Average ☐   Fringe ☐   Org. ☐   N.P. ☐

SCOUT'S NAME: HARRY MINOR   Date 4/15/84

WHITE - Office Copy   YELLOW - Supervisors Copy   PINK - Scouts Copy

JON MATLACK

JON MATLACK

Whether Jon Matlack was pitching high school ball in Pennsylvania, he had earned the reputation of being stingy with hits. By the time he graduated, he had hurled seven no-hitters and had opposing batters bringing notes from home to excuse them from having to go up against this whiz.

But when a prospect is seventeen years old, that's both good news and bad news wrapped into one. The good news is that a kid who can make it has a long career ahead of him. But most high school kids haven't fully matured. (If you question that, visit your local high school during lunch hour.) What a scout is looking at when he sees a youngster at that age is not only the kid but the kid's shadow cast forward—his potential. A scout who sees a college player when he is twenty or twenty-one has a good idea of what that prospect has to offer. It's there or it's not. But judging a seventeen-year-old calls for prophecy.

Jon Matlack's case is unique because the prophecy was fulfilled. As a New York Met, Matlack continued to perplex batters with his stuff. In 1972, his first full year in the majors, his 2.32 ERA was the best on the Mets—lower than Tom Seaver's 2.92—and he was voted Rookie of the Year. In 1973 he was third in the NL with 205 strikeouts and fourth in complete games with fourteen. In the league championship series, Matlack pitched a two-hit shutout against Cincinnati. The next season, Matlack led the league in shutouts with seven, had the third best ERA of 2.41, and placed fourth in strikeouts with 195.

Matlack again led the NL in shutouts in 1976 with six before being traded in the off-season of 1977 to Texas in a complicated and, for the Mets, unwise trade. In 1978 he led the Rangers' staff with a 2.27 ERA, the second lowest in the AL, won fifteen games and had eighteen complete games, the league's fourth best.

During Matlack's thirteen-year career he was a superb control pitcher with a lifetime average of 5.8 strikeouts and only 2.4 walks per nine innings.

All in all, Jon Matlack was a prospect who made the scouts look good.

TOM FERRICK   N.Y. METS

APR   25   1967   Date _____
(Month)   (Day)   (Year)

PROSPECT FOLLOW-UP REPORT
(Please print or type)

MATLACK   JONATHAN   Pos. LHP / BHP
(Last Name)   (First Name)   (Middle Init.)

Seen in Action _____ APR   25   1967
(Month)   (Day)   (Year)

With HENDERSON H.S. _____ Club

GREAT VALLEY H.S. _____ Club

WEST CHESTER   PENN
(City)   (State)

REGULAR SEASON _____ Tournament

Check:

☑ Suggest he be signed immediately or when eligible to sign.
☑ Suggest we look at him again.
☐ Suggest his file be closed.

Recommended for signing, fill in the following:

Definite ML prospect   Date Eligible to Sign JUNE 1967

Fringe ML Prospect   Number games seen

Start in class _____ to date _____ 2

Stop Watch Time to First Base ___ 4 5

SCORING KEY Grade on Major League Standards—not Amateur.		Present	Future	PITCHERS	Present	Future
	Hitting Ability			Fast Ball	3	2
	Power			Curve	3	2
	Base running			Control	3	2
Outstanding	Arm (strength)			Change of Pace	NONE	
	Arm (accuracy)			Slider	NONE	
Above ML Av.	Field			Other Pitches	NONE	
	Range			Field	3	3
Average	Baseball Instinct			Baseball Instinct	3	3
Below ML Av.	Pull___ Straight Away___ Opposite Field___					
	Habits			Habits	GOOD	
Poor	Aggressive			Aggressive	MODERATELY	

Follow copy to Director of Scouting. Keep white copy for your file.

(REGULAR PHASE)

Physical Description: 6:03. 195. GOOD LEGS. GENERALLY GOOD BODY. TALL, WELL PROPORTIONED. ONLY 17 YRS OLD. NOT ELIGIBLE TO SIGN TILL AFTER LEGION SEASON (SEPT.) PITCH NO HITTER. SO 15 MEN (7 INNS)

Abilities GOOD COORDINATION AND RHYTHYM. BIG MAN DELIVERY ¾ & OVER HAND. CAN ALSO SIDE ARM. QUICK ARM. FULL WINDUP. SHOWED MAJOR LEAGUE FB - CURVE AT TIMES, MAJOR LEAGUE POTENTIAL THERE FOR GOOD CURVE. CONTROL GOOD FOR YOUNG PITCHER. POISE GOOD. BODY CONTROL OF DELIVERY GOOD, ALSO.

Weaknesses: FALLS TO 3B SIDE OF MOUND. LANDS ON STIFF LEFT LEG AT END OF DELIVERY. THROWS TOO MANY CURVE BALLS FOR YOUNG PITCHER. DOESN'T HAVE REAL QUICKNESS & AGILITY FIELDING POSITION. FAIR HITTER. PITCHED WITH RUBBER SHIRT ON DURING GAME.

Summation and other comments including any information that may have bearing on his signing or not signing at this time.

DEFINATELY A MAJOR LEAGUE PROSPECT. CAN BE DRAFTED BUT NOT SIGNED UNTIL SEPT. (LEGION). WON'T BE 18 UNTIL JANUARY 68. HAS ENOUGH GRADES FOR COLLEGE. HAS HAD COLLEGE OFFERS.

What should we offer: COACH HANDLING NEGOTIATIONS. IS THINKING ABOUT $100,000. I WANT TO SEE HIM AGAIN - AND SEE HIM PITCH WITHOUT RUBBER SHIRT. SHOWED A FEW 2 FB'S.

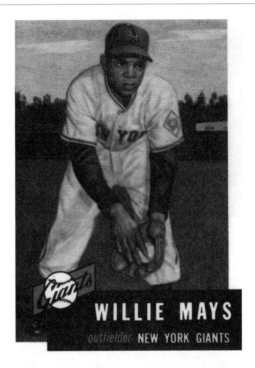

WILLIE MAYS
outfielder NEW YORK GIANTS

WILLIE MAYS

W hile Chick Genovese was manager of the Trenton team in the Class B Interstate League in 1950, he filed a report with the parent New York Giants about his young rookie outfielder.

Name of Player: Willie Mays
Date of Birth: 5/6/31
Position: CF Bats: R Throws: R Weight: 180–170 Height: 5'-11"
Playing Record: 1950 Trenton first year.
1951 Minneapolis-Giants
Sept/1950: Arm 4, Fldg 3, Rng 3, Htg 3, Power 3, Spirit 3

Major league prospect. Possesses strong arm and wrists, has some power, hits to all fields, runs good, has good baseball instinct, wants to learn, gets good jump on fly balls, has one of the strongest,

most accurate arms in baseball, should play AAA ball next year, break-
ing ball bothers him some, hits with men on, winning type of player.
Personality excellent.
Filed by: Chick Genovese

Willie had broken in with the Trenton team in late June and went hitless in
his first game. Four days later he hit his first professional baseball home run—a
grand slam against Sunbury—and his career pattern was set. It's interesting to
note that Genovese did not seem overly impressed with Willie's long-ball hitting ability. Willie's twenty-three-year record of 660 homers, placing him third
behind Aaron and Ruth, shows that Willie had more than "some power."

But Chick was right on the mark about Willie's talent for getting a "good
jump on fly balls." Watch again for the umpteenth time Willie's catch of
Vic Wertz's smash to deep center in the 1954 World Series. Also, Chick was
correct about Willie's proficiency in hitting with men on base. His career 1,903
RBIs stands as the seventh highest in baseball. Following the 1950 season, the
nineteen-year-old Willie jumped from Class B to AAA and was the marvel of
the American Association for the short time he was there. In May of 1951 he hit
.607 and inspired scout Hank DeBerry to file this report.

> May 5 to May 10, 1951: Sensational Negro boy is the outstand-
> ing player on the Minneapolis club and probably in all minor leagues
> for that matter. He is now in one of the best hitting streaks imaginable,
> hits to all fields, and hits all pitches, hits the ball where it is pitched as
> good as any player seen in many days. Everything that he does is sen-
> sational. Has made the most spectacular catches. Runs and throws with
> the best of them. Naturally, he has some faults, some of which are:
> charges low-hit balls a bit too much, runs a bit with his head down,
> there have been a few times when his manager "needed a rope," when
> he starts somewhere, he means to get there "hell bent for election."
> Slides hard, plays hard. He is a sensation and is just about as popular
> with the local fans as he can be, a real favorite. The Louisville pitchers
> knock him down plenty, but it seems to have more damaging effect
> against Dandridge and Williams than against Willie. This player is the
> best prospect in America, it was a banner day for the Giants when this
> boy signed.

Shortly after this report, Willie was called up to the Giants, beginning his
illustrious career.

Hank DeBerry had realized the goal of every baseball scout. He had wit-
nessed greatness and had participated in it by appreciating it. But he was not to
see Willie become one of the great stars of the game. Four months after sending
in his report, Hank DeBerry died.

ROGER McDOWELL

*O*ne of the most perplexing problems faced by a scout when he rates a prospect is predicting the youngster's potential—with seventeen-year-old high school kids it's a crap shoot. So it's usually safer to predict the future of a college player. Usually, but not always. Consider what happened with Roger McDowell. Kansas City scout Tom Ferrick was not impressed with McDowell when he watched him pitch for Bowling Green State College in 1982. As for the pitcher's potential, Ferrick felt that what he saw was all there would ever be and he gave McDowell an overall 48 rating. A prospect who is deemed "average" would score a 50. Note the bottom of Ferrick's report and the *mea culpa* inscription, "Missed on him."

McDowell was selected by the Mets in the third round of the 1982 draft; their first choice was Dwight Gooden. McDowell was sent to the minors, where he was a starting pitcher. In 1983 at Jackson in the Texas

League, McDowell started twenty-six games. Brought to the parent Mets in 1985, he started two games and was converted into the team's most active reliever. He hasn't had a start since. McDowell's best season was 1986 when his fourteen wins against nine losses and his twenty-two saves helped the Mets win the NL Pennant. He appeared in five games in that year's memorable World Series in which the Mets prolonged the Red Sox's autumn anguish by beating them in seven games.

In 1989 McDowell was traded by the Mets in a disastrous deal that sent him along with Lenny Dykstra to Philadelphia for Juan Samuel. Traded to the Dodgers in midseason of 1991, McDowell saw action in sixty-five games in 1992, and in 1993 he posted his career best 2.25 ERA.

When he was with the Mets, the colorful, free-spirited McDowell received almost as much attention for the playful "hot foots" he administered in the dugout as he did for his pitching.

KANSAS CITY ROYALS
FREE AGENT REPORT

MISSED ON HIM.

Overall future potential ___48___   Report No. __1__

PLAYER __McDOWELL_____ __ROGER_____ Position _RHP_
       Last name   First name   Middle name

Current Address _____
                                          City   State   Zip Code
Telephone _____ Date of Birth _12/20/60_ Ht. _6_ Wt. _170_ Bats _R_ Throws _R_
          (Area Code)

Permanent address (If different from above) _____

Team Name _BOWLING GREEN UNIV._ City _BOWLING GREEN_ State ___OHIO____

Scout __TOM FERRICK____ Date _5/8/82_ Race _W_ Games __1__ Innings _7_

RATING KEY	NON-PITCHERS	Pres.	Fut.	PITCHERS	Pres.	Fut.	USE WORD DESCRIPTION
8–Outstanding	Hitting Ability			Fast Ball	4	4	Habits _____
7–Very Good	Power			Curve	4	5	Dedication ___GOOD___
6–Above Average	Running Speed			Control	4	5	Agility _____
5–Average	Base Running			Change of Pace	4	5	Aptitude _____
4–Below Average	Arm Strength			Slider	4	5	Phys. Maturity _FAIR_
3–Well Below Average	Arm Accuracy			Knuckle Ball			Emot. Maturity _GOOD_
2–Poor	Fielding			Other			Married ___No___
	Range			Poise	5	5	
Use One Grade	Baseball Instinct			Baseball Instinct	5	5	Date Eligible
Grade On Major	Aggressiveness			Aggressiveness	5	5	__JUNE '82__
League Standards	Pull Str. Away Opp. Field			Arm Action ___FAIR___			Phase
Not Amateur	___ ___ ___			Delivery ___FAIR___			__REG.__

Physical Description (Injuries, Glasses, etc.) SLIGHT WIRY FRAME. HE IS A STRAIGHT
UP TYPE PITCHER. THROWS MOSTLY WITH ARM VERY LITTLE BODY.

Abilities   COMMAND OF PITCHES - AGILE FIELDER. GOOD MOVE TO 1B (BACK
MOVE). CURVE, SLIDER COULD GO TO M.L. AVERAGE. SLIDER BEST
PITCH BUT NOT CONSISTENT WITH IT. FB HAVE SOME MOVEMENT
WHEN DOWN.

Weaknesses   FB BELOW AVERAGE. WOULD HAVE TO BE FINESSE PITCHER.
PITCH AROUND FB.

Summation and Signability   DOES NOT REALLY HAVE ANY ONE PITCH TO
FINISH OFF HITTERS. CAN'T SEE HIS FB REACHING 6 M.L.
AVERAGE BECAUSE OF DELIVERY (ALL ARM) + PHYSICAL GROWTH
POTENTIAL.

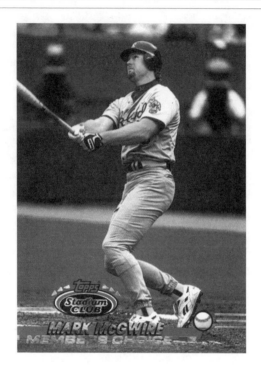

MARK McGWIRE

*M*ark McGwire was the Montreal Expos' eighth-round draft choice in 1981. But he was finishing high school and was headed for the University of California. The Expos couldn't land him. Three years later, the Oakland A's had set their sights on McGwire as their first choice, but they had to hold their collective breath because they had the tenth pick. Thanks to a tremendously rich talent pool that year, the other clubs did not pick McGwire, and when it was the A's' turn, they grabbed him and the front office rejoiced.

There was a lot of talk about McGwire when he was in U.S.C. He had tremendous power, but the long swing that Dick Bogard spotted in his Major League Scouting Bureau report had made a number of teams nervous. However, the Mets were interested in him and wanted McGwire's father to make a commitment that if the Mets picked his son, he would sign with them. Not wanting to limit his options, the senior McGwire remained noncommittal, and the Mets looked elsewhere for their top choice.

In the minors at Modesto in 1985, McGwire started knocking down fences in earnest. He hit 20 round-trippers and drove in 106 runs. After another season in the bushes, McGwire was brought up to the A's late in 1986. The following season he tore the cover off the ball. McGwire hit 49 home runs to set a record for the most homers ever hit by a rookie. That year he was unanimously awarded the Rookie of the Year honors. From 1987 through 1992 he averaged 36 homers a year. During these years McGwire was teamed with Jose Canseco to create the most frightening one-two punch of that period. With McGwire, the A's won four AL West Championships and were in three World Series, including a four-game rout of cross-Bay rival San Francisco in 1989. In 1993 McGwire missed most of the season on the DL, but he was back in 1994 battering left field seats through the league.

Thanks to McGwire, few scouts any longer worry when they see a powerful young prospect with a "long swing."

MAJOR LEAGUE SCOUTING BUREAU

FREE AGENT REPORT

Overall future potential _57.5_   Report No. _1_

PLAYER _McGWIRE,_   _MARK_   _DAVID_   Position _1B_
     Last name   First name   Middle name

Current Address _870 W ADAMS #24_   _LOS ANGELES_   _CA_   _90007_
     City   State   Zip Code

Telephone _714-745-2591_ Date of Birth _10-01-63_ Ht. _6'5_ Wt. _210_ Bats _R_ Throws _R_
   (Area Code)

Permanent address (If different from above) _2329 SIENA CT CLAREMONT, CA 91711_

Team Name _U.S.C._   City _LOS ANGELES_   State _CA_

Scout _D. BOEARD_   Date _02-13-84_   Games _1_ Innings _8_

RATING KEY	NON-PITCHERS		Pres.	Fut.	PITCHERS		Pres.	Fut.	USE WORD DESCRIPTION
8–Outstanding	Hitting Ability	*	4	5	Fast Ball	*			Habits _good_
7–Very Good	Power	*	6	7	Curve	*			Dedication _good_
6–Above Average	Running Speed	*	3	3	Control				Agility _good_
5–Average	Base Running		4	4	Change of Pace				Aptitude _good_
4–Below Average	Arm Strength	*	5	5	Slider	*			Phys. Maturity _good_
3–Well Below Average	Arm Accuracy		5	6	Knuckle Ball				Emot. Maturity _good_
2–Poor	Fielding	*	5	6	Other	*			Married
	Range		5	5	Poise				
USE ONE GRADE	Baseball Instinct		5	5	Baseball Instinct				Date Eligible _06-84_
Grade On Major	Aggressiveness		5	5	Aggressiveness				
League Standards	Pull			Str. Away	Opp. Field		Arm Action		Phase
Not Amateur	X						Delivery		_Reg._

Physical Description (Injuries, Glasses, etc.)   GRADUATION _05-85_

BIG, STRONG, POWERFUL BUILD. WELL PROP. MUSCULAR LEGS.
SLOPING SHOULDERS. WEARS CONTACTS.

Abilities
GOOD ABILITY AROUND BAG, POSITIONS SELF WELL. SURE HANDS,
AVE. ARM. @ AGG. WITH BAT, STRONG, CAN DRIVE BALL. POT. TO
HAVE VERY GOOD POWER.

Weaknesses
LONG SWING, BUT GETS BAT OUT FRONT, HANDLES IT WELL. SOME
TROUBLE WITH BREAKING STUFF. DOESN'T RUN WELL. 4.5 TO 1B.

Summation and Signability   Worth ~~_____~~
SHOULD DEV. INTO BIG H.R. MAN. AND VERY SOUND DEF. PLAYER.
APPEARS TO HAVE GOOD APPROACH TO GAME. RAISED OFF. 5 PTS.
DUE TO POWER POT.

KEVIN MITCHELL

*I*n the 1980 major league draft more than 1,200 prospects were chosen. You can look at the long list of future stars (very few) and future insurance men (many) until your eyes glaze over, but there's one name you won't find: Kevin Mitchell. Nobody drafted him, and the two reports reproduced here are the ones made immediately before the Mets signed Mitchell as a free agent on November 16, 1980. At that time Kevin was a svelte, 185-pound eighteen-year-old with a lot more hitting than fielding potential. But when someone can hit the ball as hard and as far as Mitchell can, you take the trouble to teach him how to field.

When he broke in at Kingsport in the Appalachian League, Mitchell hit an impressive .335 in sixty-two games. At that time he was mostly a singles hitter. The next season, Mitchell was injured and spent most of the year on the DL at Lynchburg. At Jackson in the Texas League in 1983 he batted .299 with 15 homers and 85 RBIs. Although his numbers at Tidewater in '84 didn't turn any heads, he was called up to New York for a look-see at the end of the season. Having seen what they thought was enough, the Mets sent Mitchell back to Tidewater, where he hit .290 and returned to the Big Apple the following season to be part of the Mets' World Championship team of 1986. That year he started showing some power and hit 12 home runs. In the off-season, Mitchell was traded to San Diego as part of the deal that brought Kevin McReynolds to the Mets in a transaction that angered many New Yorkers who had been very impressed with Mitchell's potential.

But McReynolds was already a home-run hitter and the Mets couldn't wait for Mitchell to develop. And develop he did. No longer a 185-pound teenager, he put his added bulk into his swing. In 1989, after being traded to San Francisco, Mitchell led the National League with 47 home runs and 125 RBIs. That year he was voted he National League's Most Valuable Player. After four seasons at San Francisco, where he averaged 32 homers a year, the Giants traded him to Seattle for a pitching staff. In return for Mitchell, the Giants got Bill Swift, Mike Jackson, and Dave Burba.

After an injury-plagued season in Seattle, the Mariners dealt him to Cincinnati, where he was reunited with Davey Johnson, who managed him as a rookie with the Mets.

PLAYERS STRENGTH & WEAKNESS REPORT

To: __KINGSPORT__   Date: __11-16-80__
(Manager)

From: __ROGER JONGEWAARD__
(Scout)

Player's Name __KEVIN MITCHELL__

3B	5'11"	185	R/R
Position	Height	Weight	Bats/Throws

Player's Strength   STRONG
AGGRESSIVE HITTER
AVE RUNNER
ARM PROJECTED TO BE AVE

Needs Plenty of Work on the Following:

CRUDE (DIDN'T PLAY H.S. BASEBALL)
INEXP.
NEEDS WORK ON ALL MECHANICS.
GROUND BALLS + VARIOUS PLAYS AT 3B.
CHASE BAD BALLS HITTING.

INSTRUCTIONS: If signed during season and reporting directly to team, give copy to player to present to Manager and send copy to New York Office. If signed for succeding season and reporting to Spring Training, send two copies to the New York Office.

☒ First Report   **NEW YORK METS**

☐ Supplemental   **FREE AGENT PLAYER REPORT**

Player | *MITCHELL* | *KEVIN* | *DARRNELL* | Position | 3 | B
(LAST NAME)   (FIRST NAME)   (MIDDLE NAME)

Current Address *4812 LOGAN AVE.* City *SAN DIEGO* State *CA* Zip *92113*

Telephone *714-263-910* Date of Birth | 0 | 1 | 1 | 3 | 6 | 2 | Ht. *5'11"* Wt. *185* Bats *R* Throws *R*
(MONTH) (DAY) (YEAR)   (L.R.S.)   (LR)

Permanent Home Address (If different from above) *SAME*
(STREET NUMBER)   (CITY)   (STATE)

Team Category *AM* School *METS WINTER TEAM* City *SAN DIEGO* State *CA* *JUNE 1980*
(HS • LG • JC • CL • AM • OT)   (GRAD. DATE & YEAR)

Team Name .... City .... State .... Race *B*
(IF OTHER THAN HS • JC • CL)

Scout *ROGER JONGEWAARD* | 2 | 3 | Date | 1 | 1 | 1 | 6 | 8 | 0 | Games *6* Innings ....
(NAME)   (NO.)   (MONTH) (DAY) (YEAR)

CUMULATIVE TOTALS

Date Eligible	**Prospect Rating**	**Status**		**USE WORD DESCRIPTION**	
Phase	☐ Definite	☐ Double Check		MENTAL MAKEUP *GOOD*	
Prior Draft: Last Club	☐ Chance	☐ 2nd Double Check		Habits .... *GOOD*	
Year .... No.	☐ N.P.	☐ Will Follow		Dedication .... *GOOD*	
Should We Draft?	Signed by			Agility .... *GOOD*	

RATING KEY	NON-PITCHERS	Pres.	Fut.	PITCHERS	Pres.	Fut.
8—Outstanding	Hitting Ability	2	4	Fast Ball		
7—Very Good	Power	3	5	Curve		
6—Above Average	Running Speed	5	5	Control		
5—Average	Base Running	3	5	Change of Pace		
4—Below Average	Arm Strength	4	5	Slider		
3—Well Below Average	Arm Accuracy	3	5	Knuckle Ball		
2—Poor	Fielding	3	4	Fielding		
1—Very Poor	Range	4	5	Poise		
Use One Grade	Baseball Instinct	4	5	Baseball Instinct		
Grade On Major	Aggressiveness	4	5	Aggressiveness		
League Standards	Pull Str. Away Opp. Field			Arm Action		
Not Amateur	X			Delivery		

Physical Maturity *NORMAL*
Military *NO*
Married *NO*

Overall Evaluation ☐
Future Potential

What's He Worth? | 2 |,000
(THOUSAND)

Will He Sign At Your Price?
☐ Yes
☐ No
☐ Don't Know

Physical Description (body, injuries, etc.) *MUSCULAR STRONG UPPER BODY — TRIM LOWER — NO KNOWN INJURY OR GLASSES.*

Eyes' Status: *WILL FOLLOW*

Strength *AGGRESSIVE HITTER*   Weaknesses: *INEXP*
SPEED   *CRUDE*
ARM   *CHASES BAD BALLS*

Summation and Signability: *AGGRESSIVE HITTER + PLAYER. DOESNT KNOW HOW TO PLAY YET BUT VERY YOUNG AND STRONG LONG RANGE 18 YR OLD WITH SOME TOOLS + NATURAL ABILITY. NEEDS HELP WITH ALL PHASES OF MECHANICS + TECHNIQUE. LOVES TO PLAY. NON STUDENT. HITTING APPROACH SIMILAR TO ALEX JOHNSON (DEFENSE TOO)*

COPY SENT TO

BREWERS

3B

PAUL MOLITOR

PAUL MOLITOR

*F*rom 1970 until 1973, the Brewers had no luck when it came to draft picks. Few of their selections ever made it to the majors, and those that did never became key players. Their three-year drought ended in 1973 when the Brewers selected Robin Yount as their first choice. Four more lean years followed until 1977, when Paul Molitor was their number-one draft pick. Molitor, the man Ted Williams calls "the greatest hitter in baseball today" was a college All-American at shortstop in his junior year at the University of Minnesota. But by the time Molitor joined Milwaukee in 1978, after one season in the minors, Yount was already a fixture at shortstop. So Molitor was called upon to display the versatility that has become his stock-in-trade. He has played second and third, filled in at short, and also played the outfield and first base during his career. Even though the Brewers lost to the Cardinals in the 1982 World Series, it was through no fault of Molitor's. He hit .355 and set a Series record for being the only player to ever get five hits in one game.

In 1993, after moving to Toronto where he hit .332, he was the World Series star. By batting a sizzling .500 with 8 RBIs, he led the Jays over the Phillies four games to two. In 1994, he became the Jays' designated hitter. Molitor has perhaps the fastest bat speed in the majors. He can hit with power, as his 22 home runs and 111 RBIs in 1993 prove. Molitor has been in the majors for seventeen years. How long will he go on? Ask that question again five years from now. And maybe five years after that. Even then, you may not get an answer. The following are two scouting reports filed two months apart when Molitor was in college.

MILWAUKEE BREWERS
FREE AGENT REPORT

Overall future potential **60** **$50,000.**⁰⁰ Report No. **1**

PLAYER **MOLITOR** **PAUL** **L.** Position **SS**
Last name / First name / Middle name

Current Address _____

Telephone **612 226 6672** (Area Code) Date of Birth **08-22-56** Ht. **6ft** Wt. **180** Bats **R** Throws **R**

Permanent address (if different from above) _____

Team Name **UNIV. OF MINNESOTA** City **MINNEAPOLIS** State **MINNESOTA**

Scout _____ Date **03-20-77** / **03-21-77** Race **W** Games **3** Innings **21**

RATING KEY	NON-PITCHERS		Pres.	Fut.	PITCHERS		Pres.	Fut.	USE WORD DESCRIPTION
8—Outstanding	Hitting Ability	*	4	6	Fast Ball	*			Habits _____
7—Very Good	Power	*	4	5	Curve	*			Dedication _____
6—Above Average	Running Speed 4.1½	*	6	6	Control				Agility **GOOD**
5—Average	Base Running		5	5	Change of Pace				Aptitude _____
4—Below Average	Arm Strength	*	6	6	Slider	*			Phys. Maturity **GOOD**
3—Well Below Average	Arm Accuracy		5	6	Knuckle Ball				Emot. Maturity _____
2—Poor	Fielding	*	5	6	Other	*			Married _____
	Range		5	5	Poise				
Use One Grade	Baseball Instinct		5	6	Baseball Instinct				Date Eligible
Grade On Major	Aggressiveness		5	6	Aggressiveness				
League Standards	Pull	Str. Away	Opp. Field		Arm Action _____				Phase
Not Amateur	X	X			Delivery _____				**REGULAR**

Physical Description (Injuries, Glasses, etc.)   GRADUATION _____

MEDIUM FRAME WELL PROPORTION. HAD LEG IN CAST FAST
WINTER TENDON PULLED BUT SHOWS NO SIGNS OF
AFTER EFFECTS.   **R/p 6/7A STL⁶**

Abilities FINE HANDS, GOOD FLUIDNESS. GOOD AGILITY
STRONG ARM & QUICK RELEASE. SWINGS THE BAT
GOOD AND HAS GOOD BAT SPEED.

Weaknesses HAS SOME TROUBLE WITH OUTSID PITCH & SLIDERS BUT
SHOULD HAVE NO TROUBLE WITH ADJUSTING. WIDE OPEN STANCE
AND CAUSES HIM NOT TO BE ABLE TO REACH OUTSIDE PITCH.
SHOULD CHARGE BALL MORE.

Summation and Signability I FEEL HE'LL BE A VERY HIGH DRAFT. VERY GOOD
MECHANICS IN THE FIELD AND AT BAT. COULD GO AND START AA OR
AAA. ALL PHASES OF THE GAME ARE DONE WELL AND WOULD REALLY
LIKE TO HAVE THIS MAN. GOOD DESIRE & HUSTLE & SHOWED GREAT
ATTITUDE.

MILWAUKEE BREWERS
FREE AGENT REPORT

Overall future potential **66 — $50,000**   Report No. **1**

PLAYER **MOLITOR** — **PAUL** — **LEO** — Position **SS**
    Last name   First name   Middle name

Current Address _____

Telephone _____ Date of Birth _____ Ht. **6'0** Wt. **180** Bats **R** Throws **R**
  (Area Code)   City   State   Zip Code

Permanent address (if different from above) _____

Team Name **U. OF MINNESOTA** City **MINNEAPOLIS** State **MINNESOTA**

Scout _____ Date **5-14-77** Race **W** Games **2** Innings **13**

RATING KEY	NON-PITCHERS		Pres.	Fut.	PITCHERS		Pres.	Fut.	USE WORD DESCRIPTION
8–Outstanding	Hitting Ability	*	5	5	Fast Ball	*			Habits _____
7–Very Good	Power	*	4	4	Curve	*			Dedication _____
6–Above Average	Running Speed	4.1*	7	7	Control				Agility **GOOD**
5–Average	Base Running		6	6	Change of Pace				Aptitude _____
4–Below Average	Arm Strength	*	5	6	Slider	*			Phys. Maturity **GOOD**
3–Well Below Average	Arm Accuracy		5	6	Knuckle Ball				Emot. Maturity _____
2–Poor	Fielding	*	5	6	Other	*			Married _____
	Range		5	6	Poise				
Use One Grade	Baseball Instinct		6	6	Baseball Instinct				Date Eligible
Grade On Major	Aggressiveness		6	6	Aggressiveness				**0677**
League Standards	Pull Str. Away		Opp. Field		Arm Action _____				Phase
Not Amateur	**X** **X**				Delivery _____				**REGULAR**

Physical Description (Injuries, Glasses, etc.)   GRADUATION _____

MEDIUM BUILT- WELL PROPORTION- ON SLENDER SIDE-
WIRY- LEGS ARE BOWED- STRONG BODY- NO INJURIES OR
GLASSES- JUNIOR- GRADUATES 1978-

Abilities

AGGRESSIVE HITTER THAT MAKES GOOD CONTACT- HAS FAIR
PWR WITH METAL BAT- GOOD QUICK STROKE- HAS GOOD HANDS,
MAKES DP WELL ON BOTH ENDS- ARM AVERAGE, MAY BE BETTER
NEVER HAVE TO MAKE QUICK THROW TO 1B- GOOD RUNR THAT CAN
STEAL A BASE- GOOD BASE RUNR- KNOWS HOW TO PLAY- QUICK HANDS

Weaknesses

HITS WITH OPEN STANCE AND STEPS TOWARDS 3B A LITTLE
INSTEAD OF AT THE PITCHER- SWINGS TOO HARD, TRIES TO
HIT EVERY PITCH OUT OF PARK- I DON'T THINK HE WILL BE A
POWER HITTER-

Summation and Signability

THIS PLAYER HAS VERY GOOD ALL-AROUND ABILITY- FROM WHAT I
SAW, I DON'T THINK HE IS TOO FAR OFF FROM BEING ABLE TO
PLAY IN ML- I LIKED HIM VERY MUCH AND WOULDN'T BE AFRAID
TO HAVE HIM AS FIRST ROUND PICK-

SATCHEL PAIGE

*I*t would be wonderful if we could see early scouting reports on Satchel Paige, one of baseball's all-time great pitchers. Unfortunately they don't exist. Not from the old Negro Leagues nor from the Alabama reform school in which he spent five and a half years sharpening his baseball skills. Inadvertently, the state rehabilitated Paige by not having a rehabilitation program. He spent most of his time playing ball and came out of the reform school a polished baseball player. After bouncing around semipro ball for a few years, he broke into professional ball with the Chattanooga Black Lookouts in 1926.

Paige's career in the Negro Leagues is legendary. There was no better anywhere outside of the majors. Was he better than the stars of the '20s and '30s like Herb Pennock, Lefty Grove, Red Ruffing, Carl Hubbell, or Dizzy Dean? Since Paige couldn't compete against them except in pre- or post-season exhibition games, who knows?

Okay, so what's this got to do with scouting reports? Well, we got some on Paige, but they were after he had finished—or so everyone thought—his major league career with the Cleveland Indians and the St. Louis Browns.

After leaving the Browns at the end of the 1953 season, the forty-seven-year-old Satchel went barnstorming. Then Bill Veeck again stepped into Satchel's life as he had done twice before: when he was General Manager at Cleveland in 1948 and when he ran the St. Louis Browns in 1951. In 1956 he brought Satchel back into organized baseball by signing him with Veeck's new club, the Miami Marlins of the International League.

There is little doubt that Satchel Paige was the oldest baseball prospect ever to be scouted. Here are two reports covering scouts Henry Dotterer's and Nap Reyes' apraisals of Paige during the 1956 season.

For someone who was damned with the faint praise, "still a pretty fair pitcher" and dismissed as being "smart, too old," Paige had a remarkable year in 1956. Three months shy of his fiftieth birthday, he shut out Montreal of the International League on four hits in his first outing as a Marlin. Later that season he beat Columbus in the Orange Bowl before 57,713 fans, the largest crowd in minor league history. Less than a week after that, he beat Rochester with a one-hit shutout.

He posted a 1.86 ERA with eleven wins against four losses. But the guy's fifty years old, you say. Should he go up to the Bigs? Let's wait till next year before deciding. So the next year Nap Reyes, who was the manager of the Havana club in the International League (pre-Bay of Pigs, of course) sent in another report.

Reyes's comment that Paige was "slipping (washed out)" may have been a bit too dismissive. And Nap's spelling could have used closer scrutiny: "to [sic] old."

True, Satchel didn't repeat his previous year's performance but he still finished 10–8 and had a 2.42 ERA with a fourth-place team that was under .500 for the season. However, by then Bill Veeck had left Miami, and Paige's special relationship with the team went with him. In 1958 the travelin' man went to Hollywood, not to play ball but to be in the movie "The Wonderful Country" with Robert Mitchum.

Perhaps distance does indeed make the heart grow fonder. At least it did for Nap Reyes. Although Paige didn't play organized ball in 1958, that year Reyes gave a much more positive scouting report on Paige than he had given the year before when he was playing. Go figure.

So ended the baseball career of Satchel Paige, right? Wrong. In 1965 the madcap Charley O. Finley owned the Kansas City Athletics, a team that since moving to Missouri from Philadelphia in 1955 had practically made the AL cellar their own condominium. So Charley O.—as he was affectionately called by the few who had affection for him—had nothing to lose by taking a leaf out of Bill Veeck's book and hired fifty-nine-year-old Satchel Paige to pitch a game against the Red Sox. It was like giving chicken soup to a dying man. It might not help, but how can it hurt?

So on September 25, 1965, Paige faced the Sox and pitched three scoreless innings. He went up against Tony Conigliaro and got him out and yielded the only hit to Carl Yastrzemski, a double.

So, think about it. Nap Reyes had been wrong, seven years before. Satchel Paige could still pitch in the majors, after all. But Nap, of all people, should have remembered that once a major leaguer, always a major leaguer. In 1950 Reyes, who had been a N.Y. Giants infielder/outfielder from 1943 to 1945, returned to the club after having been out of the majors for five years. He, like the prospect who was "older than his age," played in one final game. Incidentally, Nap's batting average for his last game is the same as Paige's ERA for his last game— zero.

SCOUTING REPORT
ON PROFESSIONAL PLAYER

(Please print or type his name)

Scout:__Henry J. Dotterer_____ Date of Report __8/6/56_____

Player____Paige_____Leroy__(Satchel)_____
       Last Name   First Name   Middle Name

Club_Miami Marlins_____ League __International_____

Position __P__Age__48__Height_6'4"_Weight__190_Bats__R___Throws__R__

If Player is not interesting at all, tell why not _____

_____

_____

(*Only* if Player is interesting, fill out following): White or Negro__*NEGRO*__

Major League Prospect?__No_____If "No," his Tops will be Class_____

Should we try to get him?_____What should we give for him?_____

Number Games you saw him play?_____Next year he can play Class_____

Years he has played?_____Stopwatch speed to First Base_____

His assets:_____

His faults:_____

Good habits?_____A winning player?_____Good hustler?_____

Good man to have on a club?_____Is he improving?_____Will he?_____

OVER

Has he been in service?_____ Will he be?_____ When?_____

If he won't be called, why not?_____

(Please use symbols in the following: E for Excellent; AA for Above Average; A for Average, meaning "Can get by in Major Leagues;" BA for Below Average; and P for Poor):

Hitting Ability_____ Power_____ Arm (strength)_____ Arm (accuracy)_____

Fielding_____Cover much ground?_____ Brains_____Guts_____

(Pitchers): Fast ball _*BA*_____Curve_*A*_____Control _*AA*__Poise_*AA*_

Change of pace_*A*____Slider_*A*_ Knuckler_____Brains_____Guts_____

Please give any other details you have:_____

A REMARKABLE FELLOW.
STILL A PRETTY FAIR PITCHER.

Year	G	CG	W	L	P	H	R	BB	SO	HB	ER	ERA
56	37	2	11	4	111	101	29	28	79	2	23	1.86

SCOUTING REPORT
ON PROFESSIONAL PLAYER

(Please print or type his name)

Scout: _Nap Reyes_ Date of Report _9/11/56_

Player _PAIGE ~~ROBERT~~ LEROY (SATCHEL)_

Club _Miami_ League _International_

Position _P_ Age _48_ Height _6'4"_ Weight _190_ Bats _R_ Throws _R_

If Player is not interesting at all, tell why not _____

_____

===

(Only if Player is interesting, fill out following): White or Negro _____

Major League Prospect? _No_ If "No," his Tops will be Class _AAA_

Should we try to get him?_____What should we give for him?_____

Number Games you saw him play?_____Next year he can play Class _AAA_

Years he has played?_____Stopwatch speed to First Base_____

His assets: _Good control pitcher — smart_

His faults: _Too old_

Good habits?_____ A winning player?_____Good hustler?_____

Good man to have on a club?_____Is he improving?_____Will he?_____

OVER

Has he been in service?_____ Will he be?_____ When?_____

If he won't be called, why not?_____

(Please use symbols in the following: E for Excellent; AA for Above Average; A for Average, meaning "Can get by in Major Leagues;" BA for Below Average; and P for Poor):

Hitting Ability_____ Power_____ Arm (strength)_____ Arm (accuracy)____

Fielding_____Cover much ground?_____ Brains_____Guts_____

(Pitchers): Fast ball___*BA*___Curve___*A*_____Control___*E*___Poise_____
Field – A
Change of pace_____Slider_____ Knuckler_____Brains_____Guts____

Please give any other details you have:_____

Year	G	CG	W	L	P	H	R	BB	SO	HB	ER	ERA
56	37	2	11	4	112	101		25	76			1.85

SCOUTING REPORT
ON PROFESSIONAL PLAYER

(Please print or type his name)

Scout: *Nap Reyes*   Date of Report *July 21/57*

Player *Paige Leroy Satchel*

Club *Miami*   League *I- League*

Position *P* Age *50* Height *6'4* Weight *190* Bats *R* Throws *R*

If Player is not interesting at all, tell why not _____

Slipping (wash - out)

(Only if Player is interesting, fill out following): White or Negro _____

Major League Prospect? *no* If "No," his Tops will be Class _____

Should we try to get him? *no* What should we give for him? *—*

Number Games you saw him play? *many* Next year he can play Class _____

Years he has played? *?* Stopwatch speed to First Base *P*

His assets: *Can go three or two in relief in hot weather*

His faults: *To old*

Good habits? *no* A winning player? *yes* Good hustler? *fair*

Good man to have on a club? *no* Is he improving? *no* Will he? *no*

OVER

Has he been in service?_____ Will he be?_____ When?_____

If he won't be called, why not?_____

(Please use symbols in the following: E for Excellent; AA for Above Average; A for Average, meaning "Can get by in Major Leagues;" BA for Below Average; and P for Poor):

Hitting Ability_____ Power_____ Arm (strength)_____ Arm (accuracy)_____

Fielding_____Cover much ground?_____ Brains_____Guts_____

(Pitchers): Fast ball____*A*____Curve____*A*____Control____*E*__Poise__*E*__

Change of pace__*E*____Slider__*E*__Knuckle*A*_____Brains__*E*__Guts__*E*__

Please give any other details you have:_____

Year	G	CG	W	L	P	H	R	BB	SO	HB	ER	ERA

SCOUTING REPORT
ON PROFESSIONAL PLAYER

(Please print or type his name)

Scout: *Nap Reyes* Date of Report *July 30/58*

Player *Paige   Leroy   Robt*

Club *Miami* League *I-League (AAA)*

Position *P* Age *50* Height *6'04* Weight *190* Bats *R* Throws *R*

If Player is not interesting at all, tell why not _____

_____

_____

(Only if Player is interesting, fill out following): White or Negro *N*

Major League Prospect? *No* If "No," his Tops will be Class *AAA*

Should we try to get him? ——— What should we give for him? _____

Number Games you saw him play? *many* Next year he can play Class *2*

Years he has played? *11* Stopwatch speed to First Base *BA*

His assets: *The best control pitcher in this league*

His faults: *He pitches, when he wants to pitch*

Good habits? *No* A winning player? *yes* Good hustler? *no*

Good man to have on a club? *no* Is he improving? *no* Will he? *no*

OVER

108

Has he been in service?_____ Will he be?_____ When?_____

If he won't be called, why not?_____

(Please use symbols in the following: E for Excellent; AA for Above Average; A for Average, meaning "Can get by in Major Leagues;" BA for Below Average; and P for Poor):

Hitting Ability_____ Power_____ Arm (strength)_____ Arm (accuracy)_____

Fielding_____ Cover much ground?_____ Brains_____ Guts_____

(Pitchers): Fast ball _BA_ Curve _A_ Control _E_ Poise _E_

Change of pace _A_ Slider _E_ Knuckler _—_ Brains _E_ Guts _E_

Please give any other details you have:_____

He is older, than his age

Year	G	CG	W	L	P	H	R	BB	SO	HB	ER	ERA

ORIOLES

CAL
RIPKEN   SS

CAL RIPKEN

*C*al Ripken's scouting report could be entitled "What's wrong with this picture?"

As you can see, he was scouted as a pitcher at Aberdeen Community College in Maryland. So isn't it strange that he became one of the best shortstops ever to play the game? It's unusual, but not unprecedented, for a player to start as a pitcher and later to excel at another position. Of course, Babe Ruth leaps to mind. The Babe was an outstanding pitcher for the Red Sox before he became an outfielder. In the early '30s at San Diego, a tall, skinny kid was a terrific pitcher for his high school team before he became an outfielder; he is the immortal Ted Williams. Stan Musial, who started in pro ball in 1938 as a promising pitching prospect, was also switched because his bat was needed in the lineup every day.

Going the other way was Dwight Gooden who, in addition to pitching, played third base for his Tampa high school. When certain scouts saw Gooden pitch as a schoolboy, there was a report that they weren't impressed. They thought his arm was "tired." It was. Gooden was playing third base on the days he wasn't pitching. To this day, Gooden will talk more about a hit he got than a shutout he's pitched—the sure sign of a former third baseman. Back to Ripken.

Cal's father was a coach with the Baltimore Orioles in 1976, and he knew that his son could play shortstop. Thanks to his lobbying, the Orioles picked Cal as their second choice in that year's draft, signed him, and sent him to Bluefield in the Appalachian League. After three more minor league seasons where they tried Ripken at second and third, he came up to the Orioles as a shortstop and has been their only shortstop ever since 1982. Ripken holds the all-time major league record for consecutive games played at shortstop and has been voted the American League's MVP twice, the first time in 1983 and again in 1991.

Ripken is currently the third-highest paid player in baseball at $5,711,375. With that amount, you could pay the yearly salary of every one of the forty-two United States presidents and still have enough left to buy a round of beer. And maybe the tavern.

KANSAS CITY ROYALS

FREE AGENT REPORT

Scouted As Pitcher Only.

Overall future potential ___52___

Report No. ____

PLAYER ___RIPKEN___ ___CALVIN___ Position _RHP_
Last name / First name / Middle name

Current Address _____
City / State / Zip Code

Telephone _____ Date of Birth _____ Ht. _6'3_ Wt. _180_ Bats _R_ Throws _R_
(Area Code)

Permanent address (if different from above) _____

Team Name _ABERDEEN COMM. COLLEGE_ City _ABERDEEN_ State _MD._

Scout _TOM FERRICK_ Date _5/31/78_ Race _W_ Games _1_ Innings _7_

RATING KEY	NON-PITCHERS		Pres.	Fut.	PITCHERS		Pres.	Fut.	USE WORD DESCRIPTION	
8—Outstanding	Hitting Ability	*			Fast Ball	*	4	5	Habits	
7—Very Good	Power	*			Curve	*	4	6	Dedication	
6—Above Average	Running Speed	*			Control		4	6	Agility	Good
5—Average	Base Running				Change of Pace		5	6	Aptitude	
4—Below Average	Arm Strength	*			Slider	*	4	4	Phys. Maturity	FAIR
3—Well Below Average	Arm Accuracy				Knuckle Ball				Emot. Maturity	Good
2—Poor	Fielding	*			Other	*			Married	No
	Range				Poise		5	5		
Use One Grade	Baseball Instinct				Baseball Instinct		5	5	Date Eligible	
Grade On Major	Aggressiveness				Aggressiveness		6	6	JUNE '78	
League Standards	Pull Str. Away	Opp. Field			Arm Action ___Good___				Phase	
Not Amateur	___ ___	___			Delivery ___Good___				REG	

Physical Description (Injuries, Glasses, etc.) GRADUATION ___06/78___
TALL- RANGY. GOOD ATHLETIC BODY.

Abilities POISED. POLISHED. - GOOD TIGHT QUICK ROTATION ON CURVE
ST CH ML. NOW. DELIVERY COORDINATION GOOD. COMPETITIVE
COMMAND OF PITCHES VERY GOOD FOR 17 YE OLD.

Weaknesses THROWS WEAK SLIDER WHICH HE DOES NOT NEED.
FB NEEDS ANOTHER FOOT ON IT TO BE ML.

Summation and Signability ALL HE NEEDS IS PITCHING EXPERIENCE IN PRO
BALL + GET A BIT FASTER. HAS GOOD PITCHING POTENTIAL.

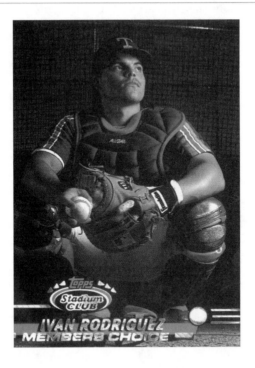

IVAN RODRIGUEZ

*I*f you look at two dates in Ivan Rodriguez's scouting report you'll see that he was just sixteen years old when the Rangers sat up and took notice. You may also note that the Texas scout watched him in two games in early November in Puerto Rico. Try doing that in most parts of the mainland. Despite the very positive report filed by Doug Gassaway, then a Ranger scout, Rodriguez appears nowhere on the Rangers' 1988 draft list because it was not until 1989 that Puerto Rico was finally included in the major league draft. Another number that is of interest is Ivan's weight when he was a teenager. He was only 165 pounds, which for a catcher isn't a lot of heft to put between you and the guys trying to run through you at home plate. But Ivan bulked up and today weighs in around 200 pounds.

In July of 1988, after he graduated and became eligible, the Rangers signed Rodriguez, and the following season he played at Gastonia in the South Atlantic League, where he showed his defensive talents by leading the league in double plays for backstops. The following season Ivan led the Florida State League catchers at Charlotte with a league leading 842 total chances. Rodriguez spent the first half of the 1991 season at Tulsa, where he hit .274 in fifty games. In midseason he got the call from the Rangers, and his expert playing in the next two seasons won him spots on the '92 and '93 American League All-Star teams. In the '93 game Rodriguez hit a double and scored a run as the AL gave the NL its sixth straight pounding, 9–3.

A seasoned vet in his early twenties, he is still developing. As long as his knees stay sound and he can learn to handle his temper, Rodriguez could become one of the game's finest catchers, thereby justifying the Rangers' confidence in him when he was a very young prospect.

TEXAS RANGERS
FREE AGENT REPORT

Monty for Indv. file

Overall future potential _____

Report No. _1_

PLAYER _Rodriguez_ _Ivan_ _____ Position _C_
         Last name   First name   Middle name

Current Address _____

                          City   State   Zip Code
Telephone _____ Date of Birth _11-30-71_ Ht. _5-10_ Wt. _165_ Bats _R_ Throws _R_
      (Area Code)

Permanent address (if different from above) _____

Team Name _Raiders_ _____ City _Puerto Rico_ _____ State _____

Scout _D. Dassaway_ Date _11/8/87_ Race _PR_ Games _2_ Innings _11_

RATING KEY	NON-PITCHERS		Pres.	Fut.	PITCHERS		Pres.	Fut.	USE WORD DESCRIPTION
8–Outstanding	Hitting Ability	*	4	5	Fast Ball	*			Habits _EX_
7–Very Good	Power	*	4	5	Curve	*			Dedication _EX_
6–Above Average	Running Speed	*	4	4	Control				Agility _EX_
5–Average	Base Running		4	5	Change of Pace				Aptitude _Good_
4–Below Average	Arm Strength	*	7	7	Slider	*			Phys. Maturity _Good_
3–Well Below Average	Arm Accuracy		5	7	Knuckle Ball				Emot. Maturity _Good_
2–Poor	Fielding	*	4	6	Other	*			Married _____
	Range		5	5	Poise				
Use One Grade	Baseball Instinct		5	6	Baseball Instinct				Date Eligible
Grade On Major	Aggressiveness		6	7	Aggressiveness				_1/88_
League Standards	Pull Str. Away		Opp. Field		Arm Action _____				Phase
Not Amateur	_✓_				Delivery _____				

Physical Description (Injuries, Glasses, etc.)   GRADUATION _6/88_

Compact type body – strong hands + forearms – well
muscled legs + back – Big Hands for his size

Abilities   Plus Arm and accuracy – catches + frames
well for a 15 yr old. Hands + feet are good. Shows
excellent bat speed – got around on 87 MPH F.B.
Should be a Plus catcher + make contact with power.

Weaknesses   Age will be against him until he
passes every one.

Summation and Signability   Worth _____

Should be signed as soon as eligible.

CHRIS SABO

W hen Chris Sabo was in Detroit's Catholic Central High as an eighteen-year-old, he was good enough to be picked by the Montreal Expos in the 1980 major league draft. But he was chosen in the thirtieth round, and Sabo elected to go to the University of Michigan, where he starred on their ball club. However, judging by the scouting report filed with the Mets, not every big league "bird dog" was taken with Sabo's talents. His less-than-enthusiastic assessment by New York illustrates the fallibility that makes a scout's job so difficult and so open to criticism.

When Sabo was once again eligible for the draft, he was chosen in the second round by the Cincinnati Reds. He signed on and was sent to the minors, where he spent five full seasons before coming up to the majors with the parent Reds in '88. By then he was ready. That year he was named Rookie of the Year and he led the NL third basemen with a .966 fielding average and thirty-one double plays. He hit .271 with 140 hits, 40 doubles, and stole 46 bases in 60 attempts. But the following season Sabo was on the DL most of the year and was only able to play in eighty-two games for the Reds.

Healthy once again in '90, Sabo made up for lost time with a vengeance. For someone who a few years earlier didn't "look to have much power," Sabo made believers of the other NL teams by belting 25 home runs and driving in 71 runs. His .966 fielding average was once again tops in the NL. In the Championship Series against Pittsburgh, Sabo's two-run homer was the margin of victory in the third game as Cincinnati beat the Pirates four games to two for the NL Pennant. In the World Series he was the offensive star, hitting an incredible .563 with nine hits, including two homers in one game as the Reds blanked Oakland four games to zip.

In 1991 Sabo enjoyed his finest season, batting .301 with 26 home runs and 88 RBIs, second only to Paul O'Neill in both categories for the Reds. After hitting 21 homers in '93, Sabo was granted free agency and went shopping for a better deal than Cincy offered him. He found it in Baltimore, but an early season injury put him on the sidelines, where he watched replacement third baseman Leo Gomez catch fire. When Sabo returned, the only spot open was right field, where he played while making his unhappiness known to anyone within earshot.

NEW YORK METS

OFP # 45

FREE AGENT PLAYER REPORT

First Report ☐

Supplemental ☒

Date of Last Report

Player: SABO (LAST NAME) CHRIS (FIRST NAME) (MIDDLE NAME) Nickname

Home Address _____ Street _____ City _____ State _____ Zip Code   Home Phone ( ) Area Code

School Address _____ Street _____ City _____ State _____ Zip Code   School Phone ( ) Area Code

Position: 3B Bats R Throws R Hgt. 5-11 Wgt. 170 D.O.B. _____

Team Name: UNIV. OF MICHIGAN City: ANN ARBOR State: MI

Date Eligible: 6 MONTH 83 YEAR Regular ☒ Secondary ☐ Grad. Date 4/84

Total Games Seen to Date: 2 Total Innings Pitched _____ DATE LAST GAME SEEN 5/8/83

RATING KEY	POSITION PLAYERS		Pres.	Fut.	PITCHERS	Pres.	Fut.	NON-PHYSICAL QUALITIES	
8–Outstanding	Hitting Ability		4	5	Fast Ball Vel.			Aggressiveness	
7–Very Good	Raw Power		3	3	Fast Ball Mvmt.			Drive	
6–Above Average	Power Frequency		3	3	Curve Ball			Self-Confidence	
5–Average	Running Speed		5	5	Slider			Mental Toughness	
4–Below Average	Base Running	4.3	5	5	Change-Up			Pressure Player	
3–Weak	Arm Strength		5	5	Other			Courage	
2–Poor	Arm Accuracy		4	6	Overall Control			Dedication	
	Fielding		4	4	Command			Coachability	
Use Major League	Range		5	5	Poise			Work Habits	
Grading Standards.	B. B. Instinct		5	6	B. B. Instinct			Off Field Habits	
Do Not Use Plusses	(TYPE OF HITTER)				DELIVERY			OVERALL MAKEUP GRADE	
or Minuses.	Pwr___ Linedrive ✗ Slap___				OH___ H 3/4___ L 3/4___ SA___ UH___				

PHYSICAL DESCRIPTION & INJURIES: Glasses ☐ Contacts ☐ Married: ☐ Yes ☐ No

REPORTED TO BE 6'. I GAVE HIM 5'11" AND HE COULD BE 5'10"

STRENGTHS: HAS SHORT COMPACT STROKE. LINE DRIVE TYPE HITTER
ARM IS AVG. FROM 3B. LOOKS TO BE AN AVG RUNNER.

WEAKNESSES: DOESN'T LOOK TO HAVE MUCH POWER. DID NOT PLAY WELL
IN THE FIELD IN THE 2 GAMES. IS PROBABLY BETTER FIELDER
THAN WHAT HE SHOWED.

OVERALL SUMMATION: DOESN'T DO ANYTHING ABOVE AVG. IS LOCKED IN AT
3B AND HE DOESN'T SHOW MUCH POWER. SHORT STROKE GIVES
HIM CHANCE TO HIT FOR AVG.

SIGNABILITY DATA: Asking for $ _____ Actual Worth _____ Agent Involved Yes ☐ No ☐

_____ START AT WHAT LEVEL: _____

PROSPECT CATEGORY: Excellent ☐ Good ☐ Average ☐ Fringe ☐ Org. ☐ N.P. ☐

SCOUT'S NAME: HARRY MINOR Date 5/11/83

WHITE - Office Copy YELLOW - Supervisors Copy PINK - Scouts Copy

RYNE
SANDBERG 2B

RYNE SANDBERG

You couldn't say that these reports were breathlessly enthusiastic about Sandberg's talent. This lack of fervor continued through the June 1978 draft, when Sandberg was chosen twentieth by the Phillies after the organization selected such future unknowns as Rip Rollins and Dean Martinez. In 1981 Sandberg was still eliciting yawns from the Philadelphia front office, having seen action in only thirteen games for the Phillies that year. On January 27, 1982, he was traded along with Larry Bowa to Chicago for Ivan DeJesus. Talk about eating your seed grain! Maybe by 1993 Phillies fans finally got over the pain of the trade when their team made it to the World Series.

Look at the reports. Neither scout, although having misgivings about Sandberg's ability to play shortstop, even suggested that he might overcome his fielding problems if he were switched to second base.

In his first year as a major league second baseman, Sandberg led the NL in assists and fielding with a remarkable .986 average. He was to go on to win the NL Gold Glove Award for nine straight years, from 1983 to 1991, and he has the highest all-time fielding average (.990) of any second baseman who ever played the game—ahead of greats like Nellie Fox, Red Schoendienst, and Bill Mazeroski. So much for fielding—admittedly not the most exciting aspect, statistically, of the game. Hitting, you ask?

By his rookie year with the Cubs in 1982, Sandberg seemed to have overcome his "struggles at the plate," his inclination to "take a lot of pitches," and his need to "be more aggressive." He hit .271 that year, and two seasons later batted .314 and was the NL Most Valuable Player. In 1990 Sandberg led the league with 40 home runs. Not bad for someone who, twelve years before, only showed "signs of bat potential at times" and was "vulnerable to high and tight pitches."

Look at the top right of the reports under the heading "Dollar Evaluation." The first report suggested that Sandberg be offered $23,000 to sign. Two weeks later, his value had eroded to $18,000. At this rate, by the end of the season, he'd owe them money for signing. But Sandberg had a rendezvous with fiscal history. On March 2, 1992, he signed a four-year contract with the Cubs for . . . ready? . . . twenty-eight million four hundred thousand dollars. It looks like this: $28,400,000, or $7,100,000 per year, which figures out to $6,647.94 for each at bat in the 1992 and 1993 season.

That a player who, up to that time, had a major league batting average of .288 was able to get into the Cubs' vault without leaving fingerprints set the avaricious club owners howling with rage. This cacophony was only drowned out by the gleeful shouts of cupidity from other stars lusting to renegotiate their paltry multimillion-dollar contracts. However, in 1992 Sandberg started to justify his ever-swelling bank account by hitting .304, and he followed in 1993 with .309. For a similar amount of money, Darryl Strawberry hit .237 and .140 in the same years.

On June 13, 1994, Sandberg called a press conference and announced that he was retiring from baseball, effective immediately. He had no intention of playing out his final two contractual years, thereby saving the Cubs over $11 million. Sandberg said his heart wasn't in the game any longer, and his .250 batting average for the year was an embarrassment. So he left the money in the Cubs' bank account and walked away. He said it was the principle of the thing. As an exercise try this: Name three people you know who would do such a thing for a principle; name two; name one!

Ryne Sandberg left baseball as he had always played the game, with dignity.

#20

V2

SCOUT _____
DATE _____

G2

NAME _Ryne_ _Dee_ _Sandberg_
FIRST · MIDDLE · LAST

SS	R	R	6-2
POS	BATS	THROWS	HGT

HOME ADDRESS _West 723 Augusta St. Spokane, WA. 92205_
STREET · CITY · STATE · ZIP

DOLLAR EVALUATION _$18,000_

TELEPHONE NUMBER _509/328-8147_

STATUS _High A_

SCHOOL _North Central H.S._
HS · JC · 4 YR.

SCHOOL ADDRESS _West 516 Augusta Spokane WA. 509/455-5220_
TEL. NO.

DATE OF ELIGIBILITY _June,_

CLASS _Senior_

_9/18/59_
DATE OF BIRTH

GLASSES— YES NO
CONTACTS— YES NO

[ ] COLLEGE [ ] JR COLLEGE [✓] HIGH SCHOOL [ ] CONNIE MACK [ ] BABE RUTH
[ ] SEMI PRO [ ] AMATEUR _____ [ ] LEGION

DRAFTED BEFORE: [ ] YES [✓] NO   CLUB(S) _____
MO./YR.

PLAYERS	P	F
HITTING	64	69
POWER	63	67
60 YARD	6.9	6.8
RUN	72	73
ARM	69	72
FIELD	67	72
RANGE	65	70

PITCHERS	P	F
ANGLE ___		
FB		
CB		
SL		
CH		
OTHER		
CON		

WORD DESCRIPTION	
COMPETITOR	good
INSTINCTS	good
AGILITY	good
APTITUDE	good
MATURITY	fair
POISE	good
HEALTH PROB.	none
INJURIES	none

PHYSICAL DESCRIPTION—DELIVERY _____

WEAKNESSES _Ryne is a stand up thrower - Does this on most every throw - appears unsure on ground balls Does not push himself to play - he struggles at the plate - takes a lot of pitches - he'll have to be more aggressive - can generate bat speed shows signs of bat potential at times._

STRONG POINTS _Ryne shows good wrist action can flip easily - gets rid of the ball when throwing. Can make plays when he has to. Really runs well from first to third._

FORM 20—10/77

121

2ND REPORT

G2

NAME: RYNE (FIRST) DEE (MIDDLE) SANDBERG (LAST)

SCOUT DATE: 5/2/78

SS	R	R	6-2
POS	BATS	THROWS	HGT

HOME ADDRESS: ___ STREET ___ CITY ___ STATE ___ ZIP

DOLLAR EVALUATION: $23,000

TELEPHONE NUMBER: ___

STATUS: GR II (Regular)

SCHOOL: NORTH CENTRAL HIGH SCHOOL (HS) ___ JC ___ 4 YR.

SCHOOL ADDRESS: SPOKANE, WASHINGTON ___ TEL. NO.

DATE OF ELIGIBIILITY: JUNE

CLASS: SR ___ 9/18/59 (DATE OF BIRTH)

GLASSES— YES (NO)
CONTACTS— YES NO

[ ] COLLEGE [ ] JR COLLEGE [X] HIGH SCHOOL [ ] CONNIE MACK [ ] BABE RUTH

[ ] SEMI PRO [ ] AMATEUR ___ [ ] LEGION

DRAFTED BEFORE: [ ] YES [X] NO CLUB(S) ___ MO./YR.

PLAYERS	P	F
HITTING	64	69
POWER	63	68
60 YARD		
RUN	72	72
ARM	71	73
FIELD	67	72
RANGE	66	72

PITCHERS	P	F
ANGLE ___		
FB		
CB		
SL		
CH		
OTHER		
CON		

WORD DESCRIPTION	
COMPETITOR	
INSTINCTS	good
AGILITY	good
APTITUDE	
MATURITY	
POISE	
HEALTH PROB.	
INJURIES	

PHYSICAL DESCRIPTION—DELIVERY: A lanky infielder with the rangy, athletic type body. If anything about his athletic actions, he may be a bit on the stiff side with a stiff back - similar to BOBBY WINE. A quiet, introvert - type individual. Has quick feet.

WEAKNESSES: Play too shallow for SS - he must go back to utilize his infield ability more. It will have his range. Also must learn to throw side-arm and from underneath. Too much over the top now. But has quick, short arm action when needed. A crude player similar to DON McCORMACK when he came out of the NORTHWEST. He will struggle with the bat for awhile — but shortstop ability should keep him around until bat arrives.

STRONG POINTS: He runs easy and throws easy. Has shortstop ability with the good hands. Utilizes a 'crouch' stance which makes him vulnerable to high and tight pitches. Stays in well at the plate and he is selective on pitches. Starts bat with a little hitching action - but it is not a bad hitch. Goes with the pitch well. Tries to have a fluid swing. Only needs time.

FORM 20—10/77

TOM SEAVER

*L*et's suppose for a chapter that you're a scout. You've heard of a terrific prospect via your network of college and high school coaches and part-time area lookouts. Now, you're aware that there are precious few secrets in this line of work, especially when it's to the bonus-minded prospect's advantage to get as much exposure to scouts as possible. In other words, you have a lot of company so you can ill afford to overlook someone who might later become a standout. Yet you have a limited amount of time to spend on each prospect and an immense amount of mileage to cover. So you devote a day, maybe two, to watching a particular ballplayer. But what if he has a bad day?

If he's not a pitcher, you can see him the next day and perhaps he will justify all the enthusiasm. If not, you have to judge him, not on performance, but on potential. Does he have power? How's his bat control? How good is his bat speed? Is he fast?

Now factor this in: Even if the prospect comes to bat ten times, what happens if he gets a couple of walks? Here's a stat for you to play with. Take Ted Williams's great year of 1941, when he hit .406. He had 456 official at bats, 185 hits, and 145 walks. Add the walks to the official at bats and you come up with 3.1 hits for every 10 times Williams came to the plate. If you saw a kid who only got three hits in two games, would you think you had seen enough to proclaim that you've just scouted the next Ted Williams? That's a long-winded way of saying that scouting is a very risky business.

It's even worse with pitchers. When you've traveled to the boonies to watch a pitcher and he has an off day, what do you do? You could wait around for four or five days until his turn in the pitching rotation comes up again, but you're not about to do that unless you're planning to run for mayor of the town. You try to get back to see the prospect later in the season. Sometimes you can make it, sometimes you can't.

Tom Seaver was seen by a lot of scouts, and here are a few of his reports. None of them are wildly enthusiastic and one is downright dismissive. On the strength of reports like these, Seaver was chosen number ten in the 1965 draft by the Dodgers. He didn't sign but opted to pitch for the University of Southern California. In 1966 he was selected by the Braves as their number one pick in the twentieth round of the January draft's secondary phase. He signed with Atlanta for a $40,000 bonus. (A lot less than the $104,000 the Phillies gave to Steve Arlin for signing. Steve who? You mean Dr. Steve Who? Arlin quit baseball in 1973 and became a dentist.)

However, Seaver never joined the Braves because the commissioner voided the deal. He had been signed after the college season began—a big baseball no-no. What to do? Finish the year pitching at U.S.C.? Tom couldn't do that either, because he was ineligible. Why ineligible? Because he had signed a pro contract. But, Tom maintained correctly, the pro contract had been voided. The answer was something like, "Hey you got your problems, we got ours." Welcome to "Catch-22" starring Tom Seaver.

Luckily the commissioner saw the unfairness of this impasse and held a special draft, just for Tom. The Indians, Phillies, and Mets all put their names on slips of paper and placed the slips in a hat. The Mets must have done something sublime that day that resonated with the Fates, because their name was drawn.

Seaver signed with New York for a $51,000 bonus. This was $11,000 more than he had signed for with Atlanta, and it almost made up for the wear-and-tear on the twenty-year-old's nervous system.

How good was Tom Seaver? He made the Hall of Fame in his first year of eligibility, with the highest percentage of votes in history. He is fourth in all-time career strikeouts and seventh in all-time career shutouts. Look up the rest—you'll be impressed.

How about the scout who didn't think that Seaver was a prospect? Now do you believe that scouting is a risky business?

Prospect Report   Scout: .....Al Lyons......................................   Date: ..May 1, 1965.....................

Seaver, Tom	Pos:– P	(Fill In If Professional)
(Player's Name)		
5009 Rancho Drive	Ht:– 6 1	Club
(Address)		
Fresno Calif	Wt:– 195	League
(City) (State)		
	Throws:– R	Orginization
(Phone Number)		
	Bats:– R	Yrs in Pro. Ball
(Parents Name)	Date of Birth:– 20 yr	Fill in when signing as F.A.
(Address)	Military 6 mtns Status:– disch.	Signed To:
(City) (State)	Married:– Single:–	Salary:
(Name of H.S.) (City & State) (Grad. Date)	No. of Depend:–	Bonus:
Univ. of So. Calif, LA, Calif June 66		
(Name of Coll.) (City & State) (Grad. Date)		

(Previous Pro Exp. If Any)

Note: Please Print All Information

Make all Comments on Reverse Side   (OVER)

Key: (E) Excellent
     (G) Good
     (A) Average
     (F) Fair
     (P) Poor

Player: ....Seaver, Tom..

Hitting											If Pro Fut Poss		If Free Agent	
Abil.	Power	Sp'd	Arm	Field	Fast Ball	Curve	Control	Change	Ext. P sldr	Poise	Field	Highest	Next Yr	Coll. Class	Prosp.
					A-G	F	A	F	A-G	A	A			Jr	res

Full Report on Ability:–   No. of times observed: ____26 inn.____

Well built boy with strong arm pitched very little in fresno junior college and then

went into service. Stays up to 3/4 to overhand fastball live and moves tendency to

drop below looses velocity. Fastball low tails off and sinks with good rotation

turns ball over to sink against LH hitters. Curve can improve has rotation but uses

it more as change at times occassinally will bust one off pretty good needs more

confidence in pitch. Relies mostly on hard fast slider very effective on lefthand

hitters when he jams them. Also pitches a little to careful at times. Good hard

PR-1 worker and strives to improve, sometimes throws palm ball for change just fair

Prospect Report   Scout: .....REX CARR............   Date: ...5/3/65..............

SEAVER, TOM	Pos:– RHP
	Ht:– 6'1
	Wt:– 195
AL LYONS TERRITORY	Throws:– R
	Bats:– R
	Date of Birth:– 20
	Military Status:– COLLE JR
	Married:– Single:– L
USC LA CALIF 1966	No. of Depend:–

(Fill In If Professional)
Club
League
Orginization
Yrs in Pro. Ball
Fill in when signing as F.A.
Signed To:
Salary:
Bonus:

Note: Please Print All Information

Make all Comments on Reverse Side   (OVER)

Key: (E) Excellent
(G) Good
(A) Average
(F) Fair
(P) Poor

Player: .....SEAVER, TOM.................................

Hitting											If Pro Fut Poss		If Free Agent	
Abil.	Power	Sp'd	Arm	Field	Fast Ball	Curve	Control	Change	Ext. P	Poise	Field	Highest	Next Yr	Coll. Class	Prosp.
					A	F	F	F	SLIDER	F	F			JR	CHANCE

Full Report on Ability:–   No. of times observed: 2

HAS A CHANCE TO BE A FAIR PITCHER. NEEDS HELP WITH CURVE.
ALSO DROPS HIS ARM TO LOW AT TIMES. HAS ENOUGH ON BALL
TO WORK WITH. WORTH DRAFT.

PR-1

5/17/65

Player: .... **Seaver, Tom** ....

Hitting												If Pro Fut Poss		If Free Agent	
Abil.	Power	Sp'd	Arm	Field	Fast Ball	Curve	Control	Change	Ext. P slider	Poise	Field	Highest	Next Yr	Coll. Class	Prosp.
					A/F	F	A	--	F	A	F				N.P.

Full Report on Ability:—   No. of times observed: _____ **8 innings**

Has the size, delivery and overall actions to be a prospect. I've seen him before at

Fresno City College; has gotten bigger but was same type pitcher. Seems to have

the velocity on fast ball plus curve. At the City College he threw a slider; against

SantaClara U he was hit hard by players I did not grade as hitters. From his

performance in this game, I could not consider him a prospect. About a year ago it

was rumored that he had arm trouble.

                         RP

PR-1

127

Prospect Report Scout: .... MARTIN Date: September 1, 1965

Seaver, Tom

FRESNO, CALIFORNIA

U of S. CALIFORNIA 1967

Pos:– RHP	(Fill In If Professional)	
Ht:– 6-0	Club	
Wt:– 195	League	
Throws:– R	Orginization	
Bats:– R	Yrs in Pro. Ball	
Date of Birth:– 1946	Fill in when signing as F.A.	
Military Status:–	Signed To:	
Married:– Single:– S	Salary:	
No. of Depend:–	Bonus:	

Note: Please Print All Information

Make all Comments on Reverse Side   (OVER)

Key: (E) Excellent
(G) Good
(A) Average
(F) Fair
(P) Poor

Player: Seaver, Tom RHP

Hitting												If Pro Fut Poss		If Free Agent	
Abil.	Power	Sp'd	Arm	Field	Fast Ball	Curve	Control	Change	SLIDER Ext. P	Poise	Field	Highest	Next Yr	Coll. Class	Prosp.
					A	F	F	A	A	A	F	chance	A	Jr	chance

Full Report on Ability:–   No. of times observed: 17 innings

A chance prospect — Dodger Draftee — If not signed we
should draft in January.

Prospect Report Scout: .... Date: 2/13/66

SEAVER GEO. TOM	Pos:– RHP

5889 RANCHO DR	Ht:– 6·1	Club	
FRESNO CALIF	Wt:– 195	League	
	Throws:– R	Orginization	
	Bats:– R	Yrs in Pro. Ball	
	Date of Birth:– 1/17/64	Fill in when signing as F.A.	
Univ of So. Calif Los Angeles	Military Status:–	Signed To:	
	Married:– Single:– ✓	Salary:	
	No. of Depend:–	Bonus:	

Note: Please Print All Information

Make all Comments on Reverse Side   (OVER)

Key: (E) Excellent
(G) Good
(A) Average
(F) Fair
(P) Poor

Buchbruk 2-13-66

Player: SEAVER, GEO TOM

Hitting												If Pro Fut Poss		If Free Agent	
Abil.	Power	Sp'd	Arm	Field	Fast Ball	Curve	Control	Change	Ext. P	Poise	Field	Highest	Next Yr	Coll. Class	Prosp.
					G	A	G	—	SLIDE G	G	G				M.L.

Full Report on Ability:–   No. of times observed: 4 Times 1965
                                                        1 Time 1966

SEAVER THREW THE BEST I HAVE EVER SEEN
HIM THROW AGAINST THE PHILIE ROOKIES A CLUB MADE UP OF PRO BALL
PLAYERS. HE HAD GOOD COMMAND OF ALL HIS PITCHES-HE SET HITTERS UP GOOD-
GOOD SINKER-SLIDER. MOVED BALL AROUND-REALLY MADE IT LOOK EASY
AGAINST BOYS THAT HAVE PLAYED PRO BALL - I KNOW AL LYONS LIKED THIS BOY
LAST YEAR - WILL GET A LOT MORE LOOKS AT HIM IF HE DOESN'T SIGN* AT USC
THIS YEAR - NEEDS SOME WORK ON CURVE BALL - NOT CONSISTENT WITH IT —
*DRAFTED BY DODGERS JUNE 1965 AND THEN DRAFTED BY BRAVES IN 1966 —
HAS NOT SIGNED AT THIS TIME - WILL BE A SPECIAL DRAFT JUNE 1966
IF HE DOESN'T SIGN

PR-1

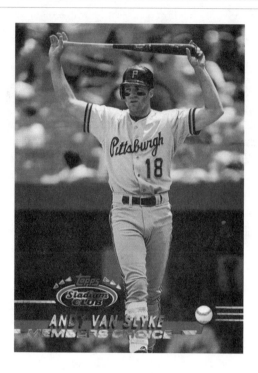

ANDY VAN SLYKE

*E*ither Van Slyke worked very hard on his fielding or the major league scouting report on him was very wide of the mark. Note that the report shows a reservation about Van Slyke's fielding ability. Then look up Gold Glove Award winners for outfielders and you'll find that he won every year from 1988 through 1992.

Van Slyke's career almost ended before it started. Drafted by the St. Louis Cardinals in 1979 when he was a senior at New Hartford (N.Y.) High School, he agreed to a $50,000 bonus. However, in his last high school game he broke his wrist, and he spent the summer of '79 at home instead of starting the climb up the ladder toward the majors.

Fully recovered in '80, Van Slyke toiled a little over three years in the bushes, coming up to the Cardinals during the '83 season. At St. Louis, Van Slyke gave little indication of the player he was to become. With the Cards in three seasons he hit .259 as against the .286 he would later compile as a Pirate. In 1987 the Cards traded Van Slyke, Mike LaValliere, and Mike Dunne to the Pirates to get Tony Pena. It wasn't the greatest trade of all time since Pena hit only .214 for St. Louis that year while Van Slyke batted .293, LaValliere hit .300, and Dunne posted a 13–6 mark and a 3.03 ERA for Pittsburgh. The following year Van Slyke led the NL in triples, tied for third place with 100 RBIs, was third in total bases and fourth in slugging percentage with .506. In the 1992 NL Championship Series against Atlanta, Van Slyke got 8 hits and 4 RBIs which helped the Pirate cause but couldn't prevent the Braves from taking the NL Championship, four games to three.

Van Slyke has shared the lead among NL outfielders in double plays with four in '85, six in '87, and five in '89. On July 7, 1992, he made a rare unassisted double play as a center fielder. Try doing that sometime. It's not bad for someone whose scouting report notes, "Outfield play can use work."

MAJOR LEAGUE SCOUTING BUREAU
FREE AGENT REPORT

Overall future potential __60.8__

Report No. __1__

PLAYER __VAN SLYKE__ __ANDREW__ __JAMES__ Position __OF__
Last name / First name / Middle name

Current Address _____

City / State / Zip Code

Telephone __315-724-6705__ Date of Birth _____ Ht. ____ Wt. ____ Bats __L__ Throws __R__
(Area Code)

Permanent address (if different from above) _____

Team Name __New HARTFORD H S__ City __New HARTFORD__ State __NY__

Scout __DICK BOGARD__ Date __5-27-79__ Race __WHITE__ Games __1__ Innings __7__

RATING KEY	NON-PITCHERS		Pres.	Fut.	PITCHERS		Pres.	Fut.	USE WORD DESCRIPTION	
8–Outstanding	Hitting Ability	*	4	6	Fast Ball	*			Habits	good
7–Very Good	Power	*	5	6	Curve	*			Dedication	good
6–Above Average	Running Speed	*	6	6	Control				Agility	good
5–Average	Base Running		5	6	Change of Pace				Aptitude	good
4–Below Average	Arm Strength	*	5	5	Slider	*			Phys. Maturity	excellent
3–Well Below Average	Arm Accuracy		4	5	Knuckle Ball				Emot. Maturity	good
2–Poor	Fielding	*	4	5	Other	*			Married	no
	Range		5	6	Poise					
Use One Grade	Baseball Instinct		5	6	Baseball Instinct				Date Eligible	
Grade On Major	Aggressiveness		6	6	Aggressiveness				06-79	
League Standards	Pull Str. Away		Opp. Field		Arm Action				Phase	
Not Amateur	X				Delivery				Reg.	

Physical Description (Injuries, Glasses, etc.)   GRADUATION __06-79__

ATHLETIC BUILD. TALL, WELL PROP. STRONG, LONG ARMS + LEGS.

Abilities

GOOD HITTING MECH., QUICK WRISTS, GOOD BAT SPEED + LEVERAGE.
CONSISTENT CONTACT. AB. Ave POWER POT. FAIR OF, Ave. ARM.
4.2 TO 1B BUT RUNS AB. AVG 1ST TO 3RD. LONG STRIDES. HUSTLER.

Weaknesses

BIG SWING, SLOW OUT OF BOX, TRIES TO PULL EVERYTHING. SOME
TROUBLE WITH HIGH PITCH. OUTFIELD PLAY CAN USE SOME WORK

Summation and Signability   Worth _____

RAISED OFF. 4 PTS AS HE HAS ALL THE TOOLS. GOOD B.B. INSTINCTS
+ PLAYS HARD. GOOD LOOKING PROSPECT.

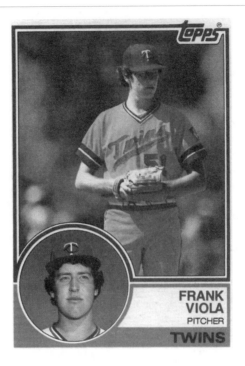

FRANK VIOLA
PITCHER
TWINS

FRANK VIOLA

*T*he seven games that Twins' scout Herb Stein saw Frank Viola
pitch told him that the St. John's University hurler had all the
makings of a future major leaguer. Viola had an undefeated year as a
collegian and had bested Yale's Ron Darling in the eleven-inning classic '81 NCAA playoff game. Yet, for some inexplicable reason, he was
not sought after by many teams and was selected by Minnesota in the
second round, making him the thirty-eighth player picked in the 1981
draft.

It took only one year in the minors before Viola was pitching for
the Twins. In his first two seasons he struggled, but in 1984 Viola bolted
out of the pack and won eighteen games, leading his team in wins and
ERA with 3.21. The following year he again was the Twins' ace with
eighteen victories for the second straight year and tying for third in the

AL in wins. After a 16–13 year in 1986, Viola led Minnesota to the world championship in 1987 with his 2.90 ERA and seventeen wins. In the World Series against the Cardinals, Viola won two games and was voted the series MVP.

In 1988 Viola led the AL in wins with twenty-four and was third in the AL with a 2.64 ERA and 193 strikeouts. That year he won the Cy Young Award. In the middle of 1989, he was traded to the Mets for five players, among whom were Rick Aguilera, David West, and Kevin Tapani.

Viola continued his dominance of batters in the senior circuit. In 1990 with the Mets he was the biggest winner on the staff with 20 victories and the lowest ERA, 2.67. He was fourth in the NL in strikeouts with 182, joining his Met teammates David Cone and Dwight Gooden, who were numbers one and two in Ks. The following season the Mets skidded to fifth place in the NL East, finishing $20^1/_2$ games out of first place, and Viola's mark slipped to a wobbly 13–15. At the end of that year he was up for free agency, and the Mets failed to sign Viola, although they had no one to replace the former twenty-game winner. He signed with the Red Sox.

In May of 1994, Viola was pitching when he felt something snap in his left arm. He was led off the field and underwent surgery that put him on the DL for the rest of the season.

MINNESOTA TWINS BASEBALL CLUB

PLAYER INFORMATION CARD	SCOUT REPORT SECTION

POSITION _LHP_

CLUB & LEAGUE _ST. JOHN UNIV_

NAME _VIOLA   FRANK   JOHN_ BATS _L_ HGT. _6-4_
(Last)   (First)   (Middle)

LENGTH OF OBSERVATION _7 GAMES_

THROWS _L_ WGT. _195_

ARM_____ ACCURACY_____

ADDRESS _106 PENGON CIRCLE L. MEADOW 11554 NY_
(Number)   (Street)   (City)   (P.O. Zone)   (State)

FIELDING_____

HITTING_____ POWER_____

DATE OF BIRTH _04_ _19_ _1960_ TELEPHONE _516-731-721_
(Month)   (Day)   (Year)

RUNNING SPEED____ BASE RUNNING____

PARENT'S NAME _FRANK - HELEN_

SPEED _5-6_

NAME AND ADDRESS OF ~~HIGH SCHOOL~~ OR COLLEGE _ST. JOHNS UNIV JAMAICA NY_

PITCHER { CURVE _4-5 SLIDER 5-6_

DATE OF YOUR GRADUATION FROM HIGH SCHOOL OR COLLEGE _06_ _1982_
(Month)   (Day)   (Year)

CHANGE _5-5_

CONTROL _5-6_

ARE YOU A MEMBER OF AN AMERICAN JUNIOR LEGION JUNIOR TEAM? ___

APTITUDE _OK_ REACTIONS _OK_

AGGRESSIVENESS _OK_

HAVE YOU EVER SIGNED A PROFESSIONAL BASEBALL CONTRACT? ___
(Where)   (What Club)

DEFINITE PROSPECT? _✓_

HAS CHANCE? _6·81 TWINS_

ARE YOU NOW A FREE AGENT? ___ MILITARY STATUS _STUDENT_

OTHER REMARKS _37_

PHYSICAL DESCRIPTION (BUILD, SIZE, AGILITY, ETC.) _GOOD ALL THE WAY ELIG JUNE DRAFT 1981_

HABITS_____

CLASSIFICATION IN WHICH SHOULD PLAY NEXT YEAR: _AA_   _OTHER SIDE_

PLAYER RECOMMENDED BY: _HERB STEIN_ REPORT BY: _Herb Stein_ DATE _MAY 1981_

AAA DRAFT — HE IS A VERY KNOWLEDGEABLE
PITCHER — GOOD MOUND APPEARANCE — MOVES HIS BALL
AROUND WITH GOOD LOCATION — HAS A GOOD LIVE
FAST BALL WITH CHANGEING SPEEDS — BALL SINKS AT
TIMES — HAS GOOD MOTION ON CHANGE UP — GOOD SPIN
ON CURVE — DOES NOT HAVE A HARD CURVE — THROWS
A LIVE HARD SLIDER — HAS ENOUGH EQUIPMENT TO
GO ALL THE WAY — GOOD COMPETITOR — WILL SIGN AS A
COLLEGE JUNIOR DEPENDING ON BONUS — COLLEGE PROGRAM
PLUS CASH BONUS AT 20 THOUSAND SHOULD DO IT —
6/8/81 AAA DRAFT BY MINNESOTTA.

Herb Stein

WILLIE WILSON OF
ROYALS

WILLIE WILSON

*B*y 1974 everyone in Summit, New Jersey, knew about Willie Wilson—he was the pride and glory of Summit High. But, at that time, he wasn't noted for his baseball skills as much as for his ability on the football field. Willie was a two-time high school All-American running back with breakaway speed.

During baseball season he demonstrated his hitting and base-running ability and drew the attention of major league scouts. But what was a speed merchant like this kid, who could round the bases in just over fourteen seconds, doing as a catcher? Nothing can ruin springy legs faster than crouching behind the plate with all that equipment on. It was fortunate for him that Willie wasn't a terrific catcher, as his scouting report indicates.

Being a two-sport star had its obvious advantages (one can't imagine a handsome athlete like this ever being lonely). But it also has a hidden drawback. Most of the major league teams knew that dozens of colleges were offering Willie football scholarships. If he really preferred the gridiron, why should a team waste a high draft choice on him? Most didn't bother. It was A's scout Al Diaz who became convinced that Willie would rather play pro baseball, and he persuaded the management that they should select him as their first draft choice in the June 1974 draft. But Willie said he didn't want to play baseball. He had heard that the minor league stadiums were the pits; the only thing worse were the long bus rides from one small town to another. No, Willie let it be known that he'd rather play football.

Enter an improbable figure: All-Star Kansas City Chiefs' linebacker, Willie Lanier. The gridiron star was pressed into service by a Royals' exec who urged him to help like a good K.C. citizen. Lanier phoned Wilson and told him that compared to football, baseball was a day at the beach. He said how the pro football owners considered their players as hunks of meat, to be stitched up, shot with painkillers, and sent back out on the field to risk serious and possible permanent injury. If he had the choice, said one of the greatest linebackers to ever play the game, he would have chosen to play baseball instead of football. Willie Wilson decided that Willie Lanier was right. He signed with the Royals. The Kansas City front office was betting heavily that Wilson would be an extraordinary ballplayer. They parted with $90,000 as a signing bonus, a sum that only a few of the first-round draft choices received in those days.

Wilson gave Kansas City some terrific years. From 1978 to 1990 he led the league five times in triples. In 1980 Wilson was high man in the AL in hits and runs while batting .326. His .332 in 1982 won the league's batting title.

It is interesting to note what Ferrick says about Wilson's attitude. It's eerily prescient. Years later, in the off-season of 1983, Wilson, Vida Blue, Willie Mays Aikens, and Jerry Martin were arrested on drug possession charges. They were all suspended for six months. Wilson was the youngest of the four, and scout Al Kubski feels that he had been the victim of company that was running in the much too fast lane. Wilson was the only one of the group who returned to play the next season with Kansas City where he hit over .300 for the fifth time in his career.

**KANSAS CITY
ROYALS
FREE AGENT
PROSPECT REPORT**

Type Prospect (check one)
Excellent ✓
Good _____
Regular Phase ✓ Secondary Phase ____
Subject for Selection JUNE , 19 74

Month _____ MAY _____

Day _____ 8 _____

Year _____ 1974 _____

PLAYER INFORMATION (PRINT OR TYPE)

SCOUT ___ Tom FERRICK

Name ___ WILSON ___ WILLIE ___ (BLACK)
(LAST) (FIRST) (MIDDLE)

Pos ___ C ___ Height ___ 6:3 ___ Weight ___ 195 ___ Bats ___ R ___ Throws ___ R

Address _____ Phone _____

City/State/Zip _____

School (HS/College) ___ SUMMIT H.S. ___ City/State/Zip ___ SUMMIT, N.J.

Date of Birth _____ Date of Graduation (HS/College) _____

Parent's Name _____ Phone _____

Address _____ City/State/Zip _____

Family Physician _____ Phone _____

Military Status _____ Draft Priority # _____ Legion Player Yes ☐ No ☐

Has player ever been selected in F.A. Draft? Yes ☐ No ☐ If yes, by what club (s) and when? _____

Does this player have any health problems? _____

Married Yes ☐ No ☑ Glasses Yes ☐ No ☑ Physical Build ___ V. Good

Is this player generally known by other clubs? _____ Can player be signed? _____

Bonus expected _____ Bonus recommended _____

How badly does this player want to play professional baseball? _____

How many times have you been in player's house this year? _____ last year? _____

PLAYER JUDGEMENT 1 (EXCELLENT) 2 (GOOD) 3 (FAIR) 4 (POOR) (Use +'s only)

Observation Period–Years _____ Games _____ Workouts _____

Non-Pitchers

Running Speed (actual) ___ 4.1 ___ Base Running Ability ___ +3 ___ Aggressiveness on Bases ___ 3
Arm Strength ___ +4 ___ Arm Accuracy ___ +4 ___ Fielding ___ 3 ___ Hands ___ 3 ___ Range _____
Hitting ___ +3 ___ Power ___ 3 ___ Frequency of Power ___ +4

Pitchers

Fast Ball _____ Liveliness _____ Curve _____ Change _____ Other _____
Control _____ Delivery OH ☐ 3/4 ☐ S.A. ☐ Loose Arm _____
Fielding _____ Poise _____ Other _____

All Players

Desire ___ +4 ___ Baseball Intelligence ___ +4 ___ Habits _____
Competitor ___ +4 ___ Aggressiveness ___ +4 ___ Body Control ___ 3

Do you have good knowledge on this player's makeup? _____

Player should start in: ☐ RL ☐ D ☐ C ☐ Other _____

KC 6A
Original to office

USE REVERSE SIDE FOR COMMENTS

SAW IN DAY GAME AT SUMMIT N.J MAY 8th

TALL GOOD ATHLETIC BODY. STRONG.

SOMEWHAT OF AN ENIGMA. PLAYED CF IN ESSEX
COUNTY LEAGUE ALL LAST SUMMER. SUPPOSED TO HAVE
ML. ARM & BE ABLE TO RUN 60 DS IN 6.6.

HIS H.S. COACH HAS BEEN CATCHING HIM REGULARLY
IN INFIELD WORKOUT. WILSON DID NOT TRY TO THROW
BALL HARD + V AT BEST IN GAME DID NOT HAVE
TO THROW ANY RUNNERS OUT.

CLOCKED AT 4.5 ON A GROUND OUT. BUT SAW
HIS SPEED IS THIN ON A 1st TO THIRD RUNNING
SITUATION. THIS PLAYER CAN RUN. CATCHING IS
NOT HIS POSITION. HAS GOOD BAT SPEED + HAS GOOD HITTING
POTENTIAL.
HE HAS HAD MANY FOOTBALL OFFERS (HELD BACK
IN SUMMER H.S) MANY BIG TIME SCHOOLS
ARE AFTER HIM.

NOT OVERLY AMBITIOUS LOOKING. PLAYS ONLY
AS HARD AS HE HAS TO. A PRETTY GOOD ALL
AROUND ATHLETE. ~~BUT ONLY PLAYS HARD~~
~~WHEN HE WANTS~~ WE HAD BETTER PUT HIM
IN SPECIAL CONSIDERATION CATEGORY. HAS GOOD
BASEBALL POTENTIAL. BUT HIS ATTITUDE +
HUSTLE DIDN'T IMPRESS ME. COULD GO ML.
CHANCE.

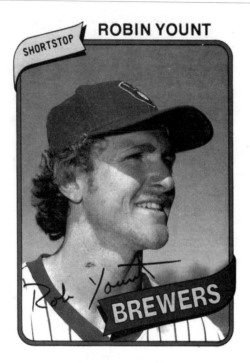

SHORTSTOP ROBIN YOUNT

BREWERS

ROBIN YOUNT

*T*here's an entire generation of Brewer fans who have never seen a Milwaukee game without Robin Yount in the lineup. He played in an average of 143 games a season for twenty years. He was the man who was always there. Starting in 1994, Brewer fans had to find another hero because Yount retired at the end of the 1993 season. He probably figured that at thirty-eight years of age, it was time to let the kids play a kids' game. But for all those years, Yount played it masterfully.

After the Brewers took him right from Taft High School in Woodland Hills, California, in the first round of the 1973 draft, Yount was signed and sent to Newark in the N.Y.-Penn League. There, he played in sixty-four games, his total minor league experience. In 1974 Yount was brought up to the Brewers. He was eighteen years old and he was to be the regular Milwaukee shortstop. It was a lot of pressure for a youngster just one year after playing on his high school team. But if Yount was nervous, he didn't show it. He played his position with great range and agility, qualities that made Yount one of the game's finest shortstops for eleven years. He was the AL All-Star shortstop in 1980, '82, and '83.

Defensively Yount led the league in two positions during his career, short-stop and outfield. In 1982, when he hit .331 and led the league with 210 hits and 46 doubles, his fielding percentage was the best for shortstops. That year he won his first AL MVP Award. Yount switched to the outfield in 1985 and in 1989 he led the league's outfielders with a .997 percentage. This, along with his .318 BA, won Yount his second MVP trophy.

Yount has a lifetime .285 BA, and despite the early talk about his not having power, he hit over twenty home runs in four different seasons. He led or tied for the AL lead in doubles and triples twice. In the World Series of 1982 Yount had twelve hits and a .414 batting average. He played a total of 1,479 games at short-stop and 1,104 in the outfield all for Milwaukee. Yount had 3,142 hits during his career, which placed him thirteenth on the list of all time great players with the most lifetime hits.

Robin Yount's absence is as good a reminder as any of the inexorable passing of time.

KANSAS CITY ROYALS
FREE AGENT PROSPECT REPORT

Type Prospect (check one)
Excellent ✓
Good _____
Regular Phase _____ Secondary Phase _____
Subject for Selection _____, 19____

Month _____ APR.
Day _____ 24
Year _____ 1973

PLAYER INFORMATION (PRINT OR TYPE)

SCOUT _____ Tom FERRICK

Name _____ YOUNT (LAST) _____ ROB (FIRST) _____ (MIDDLE)
Pos _____ SS _____ Height _____ 6:1 _____ Weight _____ 175 _____ Bats _____ R _____ Throws _____ R
Address _____ Phone _____
City/State/Zip _____
School (HS/College) _____ TAFT H.S. _____ City/State/Zip _____ LOS ANGELES CALIF
Date of Birth _____ Date of Graduation (HS/College) _____
Parent's Name _____ Phone _____
Address _____ City/State/Zip _____
Family Physician _____ Phone _____
Military Status _____ Draft Priority # _____ Legion Player Yes ☐ No ☐
Has player ever been selected in F.A. Draft? Yes ☐ No ☐ If yes, by what club (s) and when? _____

Does this player have any health problems? _____
Married Yes ☐ No ☑ Glasses Yes ☐ No ☑ Physical Build _____ Good
Is this player generally known by other clubs? _____ Can player be signed? _____
Bonus expected _____ Bonus recommended _____
How badly does this player want to play professional baseball? _____
How many times have you been in player's house this year? _____ last year? _____

PLAYER JUDGEMENT 1 (EXCELLENT) 2 (GOOD) 3 (FAIR) 4 (POOR) (Use +'s only)

Observtion Period–Years _____ Games _____ 1 _____ Workouts _____

Non-Pitchers
Running Speed (actual) _____ 4.2 _____ Base Running Ability _____ +4 _____ Aggressiveness on Bases _____ +4
Arm Strength _____ 3 _____ Arm Accuracy _____ 3 _____ Fielding _____ 3 _____ Hands _____ 2 _____ Range _____ 3
Hitting _____ +4 _____ Power _____ +4 _____ Frequency of Power _____

Pitchers
Fast Ball _____ Liveliness _____ Curve _____ Change _____ Other _____
Control _____ Delivery OH ☐ 3/4 ☐ S.A. ☐ Loose Arm _____
Fielding _____ Poise _____ Other _____

All Players
Desire _____ 3 _____ Baseball Intelligence _____ 3 _____ Habits _____
Competitor _____ 3 _____ Aggressiveness _____ 3 _____ Body Control _____ 3

Do you have good knowledge on this player's makeup? _____
Player should start in: ☐ RL ☐ D ☐ C ☐ Other _____

KC 6A
Original to office

USE REVERSE SIDE FOR COMMENTS [OVER]

142

SAW IN DAY GAME AT RECEDA H.S.

YOUNT IS A GOOD SIZE - HAS FAIR ATHLETIC BODY. RANGEY. HAS NOT YET ATTAINED HIS PHYSICAL MATURATY. 17 YRS. OLD. - 18 YRS. OLD IN SEPT.

HE IS A 4.2 RUNNER AND SHOWS SOME AGGRESSIVE - NESS ON THE BASES. HE WAS +3 ARM STRENGTH WITH (3) ACCURACY. HANDS APPEARED GOOD (2). COMES IN ON SLOW HIT BALL VERY WELL. BODY CONTROL FAIR. AGILITY GOOD. QUICK RELEASE ON D.P. RANGE FAIR. HAS SOME TROUBLE ON BALL HIT TO HIS LEFT AND IN FRONT OF 2B. CAN GET TO THE BALL BUT HAS DIFFICULTY GETTING HIS BODY OUT OF THE WAY TO THROW

I FEEL THAT HIS HANDS + ARM ARE GOOD ENOUGH TO PLAY SS. BUT THAT HIS RANGE WILL MAKE HIM JUST AN ADEQUATE S.S. WHO CAN MAKE THE ROUTINE PLAY VERY WELL.

DID NOT DO ANYTHING WITH THE BAT BUT HIS BAT MECHANICS ARE FAIRLY SOUND. SHOULD BE A LINE DRIVE TYPE HITTER WITH +4 POWER. APPEARED ALERT & IN THE GAME AT ALL TIMES. SEEMED LIKE A GOOD COMPETITOR.

HIS RANGE KEEPS HIM IN THE
UPPER CHANCE CATEGORY FOR ME.

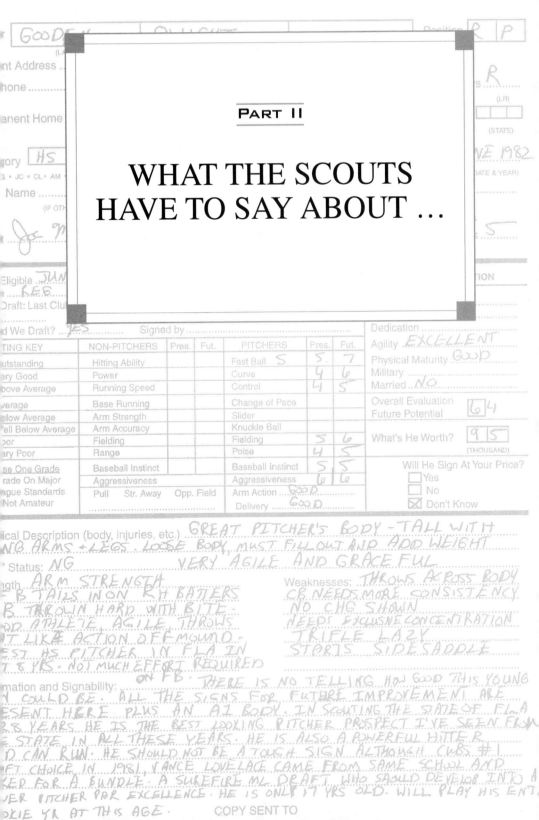

First Report

Supplemental

NEW YORK METS

FREE AGENT PLAYER REPORT

PART II

WHAT THE SCOUTS HAVE TO SAY ABOUT …

r GOODEN   DWIGHT   Position R P
(L

nt Address

hone   s R
(LR)

anent Home   (STATE)

gory HS   NE 1982
3 • JC • CL • AM   ATE & YEAR)

Name
(IF OTH   S

Eligible JUN
FEE   TION
Draft: Last Clu

d We Draft? YES   Signed by   Dedication
                                                  Agility EXCELLENT

TING KEY	NON-PITCHERS	Pres.	Fut.	PITCHERS	Pres.	Fut.	Physical Maturity GOOD
utstanding	Hitting Ability			Fast Ball S	5	7	Military
ary Good	Power			Curve	4	6	Married NO
bove Average	Running Speed			Control	4	5	
verage	Base Running			Change of Pace			Overall Evaluation
elow Average	Arm Strength			Slider			Future Potential 6 4
ell Below Average	Arm Accuracy			Knuckle Ball			
por	Fielding			Fielding	5	6	What's He Worth? 9 5
ary Poor	Range			Poise	4	5	(THOUSAND)
se One Grade	Baseball Instinct			Baseball Instinct	5	5	Will He Sign At Your Price?
rade On Major	Aggressiveness			Aggressiveness	6	6	☐ Yes
ague Standards	Pull Str. Away Opp. Field			Arm Action GOOD			☐ No
Not Amateur				Delivery GOOD			☒ Don't Know

ical Description (body, injuries, etc.) GREAT PITCHER'S BODY - TALL WITH
NG ARMS + LEGS. LOOSE BODY, MUST FILL OUT AND ADD WEIGHT
' Status: NG   VERY AGILE AND GRACEFUL
gth ARM STRENGTH   Weaknesses: THROWS ACROSS BODY
B TAILS IN ON RH BATTERS   CB NEEDS MORE CONSISTENCY
B. THROWN HARD WITH BITE -   NO CHG SHOWN
OD ATHLETE, AGILE. THROWS   NEEDS EXCLUSIVE CONCENTRATION
T LIKE ACTION OFF MOUND.   TRIFLE LAZY
EST HS PITCHER IN FLA IN   STARTS SIDESADDLE
T 8 YRS. NOT MUCH EFFORT REQUIRED
                     ON FB. THERE IS NO TELLING HOW GOOD THIS YOUNG
mation and Signability: N COULD BE. ALL THE SIGNS FOR FUTURE IMPROVEMENT ARE
ESENT HERE PLUS AN A1 BODY. IN SCOUTING THE STATE OF FLA
28 YEARS HE IS THE BEST LOOKING PITCHER PROSPECT I'VE SEEN FROM
E STATE IN ALL THESE YEARS. HE IS ALSO A POWERFUL HITTER
D CAN RUN. HE SHOULD NOT BE A TOUGH SIGN ALTHOUGH CUBS #1
FT CHOICE IN 1981, VANCE LOVELACE CAME FROM SAME SCHOOL AND
ED FOR A BUNDLE. A SUREFIRE ML DRAFT. WHO SHOULD DEVELOP INTO A
ER PITCHER PAR EXCELLENCE. HE IS ONLY 17 YRS OLD. WILL PLAY HIS ENT.
DKIE YR AT THIS AGE.   COPY SENT TO

It would be interesting if scouting reports on all the big stars were available; unfortunately they are not, for a variety of reasons. Many of the major league clubs are concerned about offending the sensitivity of their big guns by sharing reports that might contain criticisms. The Major League Scouting Bureau also keeps its reports confidential, perhaps to seem above reproach in its judgments while fighting to convince the baseball universe of its importance.

The veteran scouts have no problem with being human and therefore fallible, so we asked them for oral accounts of some of the stars whose reports were unobtainable. What was most impressive about the interviews was the amazingly accurate memories the scouts have for places, dates, and statistics. When they relate their experiences the listener is convinced that these are unique men who are true archivists of the sport.

MOISES ALOU

Scout Lenny Yochim: "I cross-checked him when he was in a junior college in Northern California. I think he was involved in something like the Fellowship of Christian Athletes. He played center field, and our area scout at that time, Bart Braun (who is now with Atlanta), was high on him and so Pittsburgh drafted him in the first round of the '86 draft. He was quite a talent, a good looking ballplayer. He had the tools, the equipment. He could run, throw, field, hit; all the potentials. He was a 6.7 runner in the sixty-yard dash. That's one of the things that the Pirates were known for, running speed. That goes all the way back to the Branch Rickey days. The sixty-yard dash was the big thing with the St. Louis Cardinals, Brooklyn Dodgers, and the Pirates. Alou had good bat speed. We signed him."

ALBERT BELLE

Scout Tom Giordano: "I remember he played right field for L.S.U. [Louisiana State University] when I saw him in 1986. His baseball tools and ability were outstanding and, even though he didn't appear to be a team player, we knew he had the stuff to make it. The change around that he did was remarkable. I can tell you an interesting story about that. At the Indians' spring training in '90, the Cleveland manager, John McNamara, didn't like the kid's shenanigans. Belle wouldn't run out grounders and generally dogged it [so] McNamara had him sent down to Triple A ball. But the kid had so much potential that the Indians didn't give up on him. Danny O'Dowd, the director of baseball operations, and John Hart of the Indians' organization took Belle under their wing in the fall and winter of 1991, brought him to Cleveland, and got him an off-season job. They watched him, counseled the kid, and turned him around. From then on, Belle became a team player and today is one of the biggest stars in the majors. You like to be able to tell stories like that. Give credit to Danny O'Dowd and John Hart."

ANDY BENES

Scout Tom Giordano: "I saw him when he was at the University of Evansville. He was a tall right-hander with a good fastball and snappy curve. As a cross-checker, I could see why the area scout had turned him in as a high draft possibility. But in '88 the Indians' priority was a middle infielder, and we passed up Benes to take Mark Lewis. Jack McKeon, the general manager of the Padres, was also at the game and he stayed for three innings. As he left, he winked at me, indicating that San Diego would go for Benes."

LENNY DYKSTRA

Scout Harry Minor: "The Mets didn't have me cross-check him because of his size. When I saw him I couldn't believe it. I thought Dykstra was the bat boy. But he did everything. He outran everybody, outthrew everybody, and was just very impressive. [Scout] Joe McIlvaine was at that workout, and he was impressed. Darrin Jackson is another player we had at that workout. Dykstra really attracted our attention, no matter what his size was. Something else about him: We never sent high school players to Class 'A' ball, we sent them to the Rookie League. Dykstra said, 'I'm not going to the Rookie

League. If I can't play "A" ball, I'm not signing.' He was that cocky. We did get a commitment from him that if he didn't get off to a good start then he would agree to go to the Rookie League. He went to Shelby [South Atlantic League] and hit about .270. Two years later he led the Carolina League in everything. He had all the confidence in the world. In high school he never got thrown out stealing bases. [pause] I don't like talking about how much the Mets miss him in New York."

CECIL FIELDER

Scout Tom Ferrick: "He came from California and he had only one skill, swinging the bat. We [Kansas City] traded him to Toronto for somebody. He went to Japan and had a good year and on the basis of that the Tigers signed him as a free agent. Playing in the Japanese leagues brought him into the limelight."

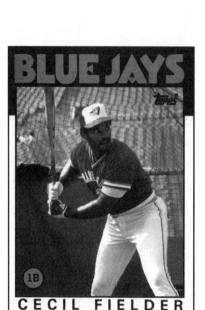

CECIL FIELDER

Mets Scout Harry Minor: "I saw him in a workout when he was in high school in '81. He was about as big then as he is now. Lenny Dykstra was also at the workout. You can imagine Dykstra, a 135-pound little kid, standing next to Cecil Fielder. Cecil was a 'one-tool guy.' If he didn't hit he couldn't play at all. Toronto gave up on him as a hitter. He went over to Japan and became more patient at the plate because over there they throw breaking pitches, and it helped him a great deal."

ANDRES GALARRAGA

Scout Howie Haak: "I saw him play in Venezuela in '78 in one of the leagues down there. He was just a kid, maybe eighteen. At the time, I wasn't impressed. I didn't want to sign him, but Montreal did in '79 and sent some ballplayers they had under contract to Venezuela for Galarraga. He developed into one of the finest fielding first basemen in baseball."

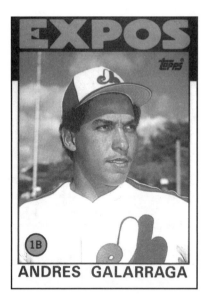

TOM GLAVINE

Len Merullo: "Ah, what a kid. From my area [Massachusetts]. A class act. I saw him in the Major League Tryout Camp when he was in high school. We didn't know if he was going to play baseball or hockey. He was a great hockey player and had a four-year scholarship to the University of Lowell. When I met his folks and wanted to find out if he would go in that year's draft or go to Lowell, Tom did all the talking. He handled himself beautifully. This seventeen-year-old kid. After the interview I was sure that he wanted to play baseball."

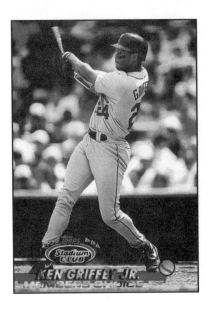

KEN GRIFFEY, JR.

Scout Tom Giordano: "I went to see Griffey when he was at Moeller High School in Cincinnati. When the area scout, Bill Lawlor, picked me up at the airport, he said that if the Indians ever, ever would draft a kid out of high school as their number one, this was the kid. He was the best young player he had ever scouted. Scouts always try to pump their players up and that's good. When I saw Griffey playing center field, I wasn't impressed. He didn't get a jump on the ball and seemed a little lazy out there. But when he got up to bat—Wow!—You had to fall in love with him right then and there. He had trouble in high school; he wrecked a couple of cars, but he had outgrown that kind of stuff. He has a great respect and a great love for his dad [with whom he played in '90 and '91 at Seattle to form the only father/son player combination in major league history]."

BO JACKSON

Pittsburgh Pirate scout Lenny Yochim: "He was a sprinter playing center field at Auburn. You didn't get a chance to see him play too much. In the three-game series I saw him, I saw everything you were supposed to see in a ballplayer. He had everything. At that time, Jackson was limited as to the amount of baseball he played because of football. He never played spring sports until football was over and didn't get involved in summer baseball. I didn't see him in high school, but they said that if track and baseball were on at the same time, he would pick track over baseball. Jackson and Frank Thomas played on the same team for a year. Jackson was drafted in '86, Thomas in '89."

GREGG JEFFERIES

Scout Harry Minor: "Most scouts didn't think he was big enough. I went up to see him play in high school near San Francisco and I saw him play two games. He was a shortstop and the big question was, what position he should be playing? Maybe you can see too much of a kid because most of the area scouts were turned off on Jefferies. I was just very impressed with him. They had a workout up at Berkeley for the outstanding high school players, and he was picked on the team to represent Northern California to play against Southern California in an All-Star game. In the workout Gregg Jefferies did everything. He wouldn't sit still. He wanted to go out and run for the coaches or play another position. He was very impressive with his desire to play the game. And there wasn't any question in my mind that he had a chance to hit. When you get a guy in middle infield who can hit you just got to go for him. We were twentieth in the '85 draft and McIlvaine wanted a pitcher from Washington and I wanted Jefferies. I didn't think we were going to get him, but he was still there when our turn came up."

Scout Tom Ferrick: "We had him at Kansas City from the Mets, but we had Wally Joyner signed and the only place Jefferies could play was first base. We traded him to the Cards. But we always knew that he was going to make it big. The one thing about him is that he plays hard."

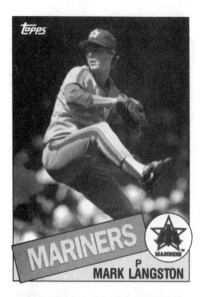

MARK LANGSTON

Scout Harry Minor: "I saw him when he played in college at San Jose. In the game I saw him he had a very bad day. Langston wasn't throwing well at all. I went back the second time and he threw better. His curve ball was by far his best pitch. But he didn't throw as hard as I would have liked him to throw. [laugh] It's the only mistake I ever made."

Scout Howie Haak: "At San Jose State I saw him pitch a shutout and he looked very good. We were interested, but then we heard that he had hurt his arm so we passed on him."

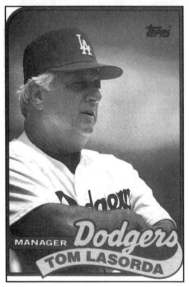

TOMMY LASORDA

Scout Tom Ferrick: "I didn't sign him. Jocko Collins, who used to scout for the Phillies signed him. He was local, [from] Norristown, Pennsylvania. He got practically nothing to sign. He was in the Phillies' organization quite awhile and later on he surfaces as a manager with the Dodger organization. As a matter of fact he pitched for Montreal. He finally succeeded Walter Alston as Dodger manager. He's a wonderful guy." (In Montreal he led the International League in wild pitches with fourteen in 1953, not quite living up to his high-water mark of twenty wild pitches when he led the Can-Am league in that department in 1948. Going with what he could do best, Tommy shares the NL record for most wild pitches in an inning with the three he tossed away in 1955.)

Scout Tom Giordano: "I remember he had a spitball. He'd turn the ball over, and he probably had a piece of emery board and some Vaseline under his belt. He got into the big leagues as a manager. A terrific guy."

DON MATTINGLY

DON
MATTINGLY

Jax Robertson, former Yankee scout who is now with the Florida Marlins: "When Don was in Memorial High School in Evansville, Indiana, he was scouted by the Major League Scouting Bureau. I followed up for the Yankees. Don had fine speed and a good throwing arm. He was a great hitter and had a great eye. I saw him play two games before the draft, and the reason why there weren't all that many teams interested in him was because the word was out that he wanted a lot of money to sign.

"After we drafted him, his school was in the state finals and he kept playing and I kept going back to watch him. He just got better and better and more impressive. I was hoping, well not exactly hoping, that his team would finally lose so I could sit down with him and his parents and talk about signing with the Yankees. But they kept winning and finally, at the end of June, they won the championship. I'm glad I was with the Yankees at the time because they went along with Mattingly's demands and we gave him the money we would ordinarily give to a third or fourth round draft choice. Don was selected nineteenth [493rd pick overall].

"Don didn't want to go to college and play ball there because he didn't feel that college ball was challenging enough for him. Instead, he wanted to get to the majors as fast as he could, so he signed with the Yankees just after his eighteenth birthday."

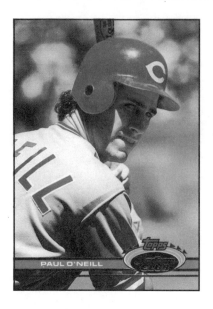

PAUL O'NEILL

Scout Len Merullo: "I saw him play in the Eastern League at Waterbury in '83. He was a fiery, fiery guy. I remember once in Burlington, Vermont, in '84 he gets called up as the last out in the ball game. He hits a shot to the left of shortstop. The fielder made a good play and threw him out. But it was a real bad call; he was absolutely safe. And he's about twenty feet past first base, figuring he's got a base hit, and he turns around and sees that everybody's going off the field. He charges up to the umpire who called him out and starts shouting at him. Here's this gangly guy looking down at the umpire who just wouldn't give. They had to call the cops to separate them."

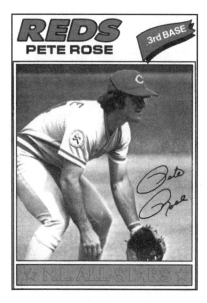

PETE ROSE

Scout Tom Ferrick: "I turned in a report on him from the Instructional League way back when. He went to Western High School in Cincinnati, which is one of the hotbeds of baseball players. His uncle was a scout for the Reds, Bernie Bierbauer. He signed him. The day I saw him he was playing left field and I remember saying that this young man has limited skills and he's going to have to find some way to play in the big leagues. I didn't know he was going to be that good."

Scout Lenny Merullo: "I saw him play when he was seventeen, in 1958. He played second base and hit about .240. He was 5'8" and weighed about 150 pounds. We had to grade the players as to how high we thought they would go—majors, triple A, et cetera. I put down, 'No higher than A ball.' But then again, nobody else thought that he would make it. He actually made himself a ballplayer. It's a great thing to see something like that. How wrong a scout can be if a boy really puts effort into it."

MIKE SCHMIDT

Scout Tom Ferrick: "I didn't scout him because at the time, he was about to be drafted by Philadelphia. He went to Ohio University. He had two bad knees, and everybody kind of shied away from him. The only one who really stayed with him was a scout by the name of Tony Lucadello, who was a famous scout for the Phillies. Tony sent fifty players to the big leagues. Schmidt's knees came around and he became quite a ballplayer. A sure Hall of Famer."

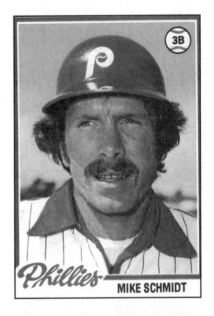

MIKE SCHMIDT

GARY SHEFFIELD

Scout Tom Giordano: "I saw him play when he was in high school in Tampa—Hillsborough High, I think. You immediately saw an outstanding arm. His bat speed was the quickest I'd seen for a long time. He paralleled Manny Ramirez, the way the ball jumps off the bat. I still give the edge to our guy Manny. Sheffield was definitely a number one pick. We would have taken him, but Milwaukee was ahead of us. He was a shortstop at the time, good hands, good arm, and a plus runner. He hit with power. He's the nephew of Dwight Gooden."

FRANK THOMAS

Scout Lenny Merullo: "I saw him play in the Cape Cod League in '88. He played on the same team as J. T. Snow. One was an outstanding first baseman and the other was an outstanding hitter. Frank really had problems fielding back then. He's still not the greatest fielder, but he can hit the ball a long way. I remember talking to him and he said, 'Call my dad. He'll tell you all about me.' In the All-Star game of the Cape Cod League that year there was a home-run hitting contest. Frank won it. At that time there was a question whether he was going to play pro baseball or stay at Auburn and play football."

Scout Lenny Yochim: "I saw both Frank Thomas and Bo Jackson. They were both outstanding talents. Thomas, to me, was a premium draft player. He has a quality bat, had power, and at that time he had good running speed. He wasn't as large as he is now and I guess you could say that his mobility has been hindered by his added size. But now he can take all the time he wants running around the bases after hitting those home runs."

NEW YORK METS

FREE AGENT PLAYER REPORT

OFP # 48

port ☐
nental ☒

Date of Last Report

er AiKM
(LAST)

e Address

ol Address

tion: RHP-S

n Name: He

Eligible: 5/84

Games Seen   5/3/84

ATING KEY   LITIES
standing
Good
ve Average
rage
w Average
ak

PART III

THE FOUR THAT GOT AWAY

	Arm Accuracy	4	5	Overall Control		Dedication
	Fielding	3	4	Command		Coachability
Major League	Range	4	3	Poise		Work Habits
ng Standards.	B. B. Instinct	5	6	B. B. Instinct		Off Field Habits

t Use Plusses
r Minuses.

(TYPE OF HITTER)   Pwr ☒ Linedrive ___ Slap ___

DELIVERY   OH ___ H 3/4 ___ L 3/4 ___ SA ___ UH ___

OVERALL MAKEUP GRADE

CAL DESCRIPTION & INJURIES: Glasses ☐   Contacts ☐   Married: ☐ Yes ☐ No

HANDS. LONG ARMS. HEAVY LEGS AND ANKLES. HERMAN MUNSTER
DY.

GTHS. PHYSICAL STRENGTH. SHOULD HAVE AVG ARM. AGILE FOR
E. HAS SHORT STROKE AND GOES INTO BALL GOOD.

ESSES: MAY RUN 4.4 BUT THAT WOULD BE VERY BEST. LABORS
2UN. WILL ONLY GET SLOWER. IS A FRONT FOOT HITTER. ONLY HITTING
HIS ARMS. POSITION IS IN QUESTION. NO WAY WILL HE HAVE RANGE TO PLAY S

LL SUMMATION: SAW HIM PITCH AND PLAY SS. DART THROWER AS PITCHER
82. TOPS. NO BR. PITCH. DOESN'T HAVE POWER STROKE BUT
SO STRONG HE WILL HIT WITH SOME POWER

BILITY DATA: Asking for $ [   ]   Actual Worth 25.000   Agent Involved   Yes ☐   No ☐

SICAL STRENGTH MAKES HIM WORTHWHILE. UNDERSTAND HE HAS
T BALL SC. AT OK.U. DOESN'T HAVE BASEBALL
ILITY TO COMPETE WITH FOOTBALL   START AT WHAT LEVEL: [   ]

ECT CATEGORY: Excellent ☐   Good ☐   Average ☒   Fringe ☐   Org. ☐   N.P. ☐

'S NAME: HARRY MINOR   Date 5/3/84

WHITE - Office Copy   YELLOW - Supervisor's Copy   PINK - Scout's Copy

TROY AIKMAN,
JOHN ELWAY,
JAY SCHROEDER,
AND
DEION SANDERS

Mention these names and you feel that fall is in the air. But we're not talking football in a book about baseball. We're talking about baseball players. And that's who these guys were and one still is. Of the four, Troy Aikman was the least promising baseball prospect when he was in high school in Oklahoma. Mets scout Harry Minor saw him and filed his report. A Herman Munster body? There's nothing that will turn off scouts faster than a shortstop who can't run and a pitcher who can't throw hard. Troy wasn't drafted as a high schooler, so he went to the University of Oklahoma and began his football career. He later transferred to U.C.L.A. and was a brilliant quarterback. Baseball was all but forgotten by 1989 when he was signed by the Dallas Cowboys. By 1992 Troy was the NFL's number-one passer with 302 completions and in 1993 he led the Cowboys to Super Bowl XXVII. In that rout, Troy completed 22 of 30 passes for four touchdowns and 273 yards to stomp all over the Buffalo Bills, 52–17 for the Championship.

NEW YORK METS

FREE AGENT PLAYER REPORT

OFP # 48

First Report ☐
Supplemental ☒

				Date of Last Report	

Player: AIKMAN (LAST NAME) | TROY (FIRST NAME) | (MIDDLE NAME) | Nickname

Home Address _____ Street _____ City _____ State _____ Zip Code | Home Phone ( ) Area Code

School Address _____ Street _____ City _____ State _____ Zip Code | School Phone ( ) Area Code

Position: RHP-SS Bats R Throws R Hgt. 6-4 Wgt. 195 D.O.B. _____

Team Name: HENRYETTA H.S. City: HENRYETTA State: OKLA

Date Eligible: 6 84 MONTH YEAR Regular ☒ Secondary ☐ Grad. Date 5/84

Total Games Seen to Date: 1 Total Innings Pitched _____ DATE LAST GAME SEEN 5/3/84

RATING KEY	POSITION PLAYERS	Pres.	Fut.	PITCHERS	Pres.	Fut.	NON-PHYSICAL QUALITIES
8–Outstanding	Hitting Ability	3	4	Fast Ball Vel.			Aggressiveness
7–Very Good	Raw Power	4	5	Fast Ball Mvmt.			Drive
6–Above Average	Power Frequency	3	4	Curve Ball			Self-Confidence
5–Average	Running Speed	4	3	Slider			Mental Toughness
4–Below Average	Base Running 4.4½	4	3	Change-Up			Pressure Player
3–Weak	Arm Strength	4	5	Other			Courage
2–Poor	Arm Accuracy	4	5	Overall Control			Dedication
	Fielding	3	4	Command			Coachability
Use Major League	Range	4	3	Poise			Work Habits
Grading Standards.	B. B. Instinct	5	6	B. B. Instinct			Off Field Habits
Do Not Use Plusses	(TYPE OF HITTER)			DELIVERY			OVERALL MAKEUP GRADE
or Minuses.	Pwr ✗ Linedrive ___ Slap ___			OH ___ H 3/4 ___ L 3/4 ___ SA ___ UH ___			

PHYSICAL DESCRIPTION & INJURIES: Glasses ☐ Contacts ☐ Married: ☐ Yes ☐ No
BIG HANDS. LONG ARMS. HEAVY LEGS AND ANKLES. HERMAN MUNSTER BODY.

STRENGTHS: PHYSICAL STRENGTH. SHOULD HAVE AVG ARM. AGILE FOR SIZE. HAS SHORT STROKE AND GOES INTO BALL GOOD.

WEAKNESSES: MAY RUN 4.4 BUT THAT WOULD BE VERY BEST. LABORS TO RUN. WILL ONLY GET SLOWER. IS A FRONT FOOT HITTER. ONLY HITTING WITH HIS ARMS. POSITION IS IN QUESTION. NO WAY WILL HE HAVE RANGE TO PLAY SS.

OVERALL SUMMATION: SAW HIM PITCH AND PLAY SS. DART THROWER AS PITCHER 81-82 TOPS. NO BR. PITCH. DOESN'T HAVE POWER STROKE BUT IS SO STRONG HE WILL HIT WITH SOME POWER.

SIGNABILITY DATA: Asking for $ _____ Actual Worth 25,000 Agent Involved Yes ☐ No ☐
PHYSICAL STRENGTH MAKES HIM WORTHWHILE. UNDERSTAND HE HAS FOOTBALL SC. AT OK.U. DOESN'T HAVE BASEBALL ABILITY TO COMPETE WITH FOOTBALL START AT WHAT LEVEL: _____

PROSPECT CATEGORY: Excellent ☐ Good ☐ Average ☒ Fringe ☐ Org. ☐ N.P. ☐

SCOUT'S NAME: HARRY MINOR Date 5/3/84

WHITE - Office Copy   YELLOW - Supervisors Copy   PINK - Scouts Copy

■ ■ ■

John Elway is a different story. His first love was baseball, and in high school he hit a robust .491 in 1979 in his senior year. As if that weren't enough, he also pitched. Kansas City drafted him in their eighteenth round, but he went to Stanford on a football scholarship instead. In 1981, when he was a junior and therefore eligible for the draft once more, the Yankees selected him in the second round. Elway was actually New York's primary choice, because their first-round pick had been ceded to San Diego when the Yankees took former Padres' free agent Dave Winfield. Elway signed with the Yankees for a $140,000 bonus and was sent to Oneonta in 1982 for a short season. There, he hit .318 in 42 games with four homers and thirteen stolen bases.

In 1983 pro football tapped Elway, and he was drafted by the Baltimore Colts. He refused to sign with Baltimore, and the Colts traded their rights to Elway to Denver. He signed with the Broncos for one of the most lucrative contracts in pro football history. That was the end of his baseball career, even though Yankee owner George Steinbrenner reportedly offered Elway a half-million dollar yearly salary to play in the Yankee organization. One doubts that George is a Denver Bronco fan, especially since there is no indication that John ever returned any part of his original $140,000 bonus. That figures out to $3,333 for every game he played in Class A ball.

MAJOR LEAGUE SCOUTING BUREAU
FREE AGENT REPORT

Overall future potential **54.5**   Report No. **1**

PLAYER **ELWAY** (Last name)   **JOHN** (First name)   **ALBERT** (Middle name)   Position **OF**

Current Address **19151 TULSA**   **NORTHRIDGE** (City)   **CALIF** (State)   **91326** (Zip Code)

Telephone **213-360-6234** (Area Code)   Date of Birth **06-28-60** Ht. **6'3** Wt. **185** Bats **L** Throws **R**

Permanent address (if different from above) **Same**

Team Name **GRANADA HILLS H.S.** City **GRANADA HILLS** State **CALIF**

Scout **DICK BOGARD**   Date **04-19-79** Race **WHITE** Games **1**   Innings **7**

RATING KEY	NON-PITCHERS		Pres.	Fut.	PITCHERS		Pres.	Fut.	USE WORD DESCRIPTION
8—Outstanding	Hitting Ability	*	3	5	Fast Ball	*			Habits **good**
7—Very Good	Power	*	5	6	Curve	*			Dedication **good**
6—Above Average	Running Speed	*	5	5	Control				Agility **good**
5—Average	Base Running		4	5	Change of Pace				Aptitude **good**
4—Below Average	Arm Strength	*	5	6	Slider	*			Phys. Maturity **excellent**
3—Well Below Average	Arm Accuracy		4	5	Knuckle Ball				Emot. Maturity **good**
2—Poor	Fielding	*	4	5	Other	*			Married **no**
	Range		5	5	Poise				
Use One Grade	Baseball Instinct		4	5	Baseball Instinct				Date Eligible **06-79**
Grade On Major	Aggressiveness		5	5	Aggressiveness				
League Standards	Pull Str. Away		Opp. Field		Arm Action				Phase **Reg**
Not Amateur	X				Delivery				

Physical Description (Injuries, Glasses, etc.)   GRADUATION **06-79**
SUPER BODY, TALL, WELL PROP. LONG ARMS & LEGS, GOOD ATHLETIC BUILD

Abilities
SHORT SWING, GOOD BAT SPEED & LEVERAGE. MAKES CONSISTANT CONTACT, HAS SOME POWER. POT. TO HAVE AB. AVE. ARM STRENGTH AVE. RUNNER, FAIR INSTINCTS, GOOD ATHLETE.

Weaknesses
HOLDS BAT TOO FAR FOREWARD, ALMOST STARTS WITH STILL BAT, NEEDS TO GET SOME MOMENTUM GOING PRIOR TO SWING. WITH SOME MINOR ADJUSTMENTS HAS CHANCE TO BECOME GOOD HITTER.

Summation and Signability   Worth _____
PITCHED ON DAY SCOUTED, COULD BE PROSPECT ON ARM STRENGTH ALONE BUT NO BREAKING STUFF OR KNOWLEDGE OF PITCHING. OUTSTANDING FB QUARTERBACK. SCHOLARSHIP TO STANFORD UNIV.

With Denver, Elway has twice led the NFL in completions and has been in three Super Bowls without winning one. In the 1987 game he completed 22 of 37 passes when Denver lost to the New York Giants. The Big Apple finally got a measure of revenge for having been spurned by a potential Yankee baseball star.

■　■　■

MAJOR LEAGUE SCOUTING BUREAU
FREE AGENT REPORT

Overall future potential __60.7__ Report No. __1__

PLAYER __SCHROEDER__ (Last name) __JAY__ (First name) __BRIAN__ (Middle name) Position __C__

Current Address __789 SWARTHMORE AVE__ __PACIFIC PALISADES__ (City) __CALIF__ (State) __90272__ (Zip Code)

Telephone __213-459-3687__ (Area Code) Date of Birth __06-28-61__ Ht. __6'4__ Wt. __200__ Bats __R__ Throws __R__

Permanent address (if different from above) __SAME__

Team Name __PALISADES H.S.__ City __PACIFIC PALISADES__ State __CALIF__

Scout __DICK BOGARD__ Date __15-15-79__ Race __WHITE__ Games __1__ Innings __7__

RATING KEY	NON-PITCHERS		Pres.	Fut.	PITCHERS		Pres.	Fut.	USE WORD DESCRIPTION
8–Outstanding	Hitting Ability	*	4	5	Fast Ball	*			Habits __good__
7–Very Good	Power	*	4	6	Curve	*			Dedication __good__
6–Above Average	Running Speed	*	5	5	Control				Agility __good__
5–Average	Base Running		4	5	Change of Pace				Aptitude __good__
4–Below Average	Arm Strength	*	6	6	Slider	*			Phys. Maturity __excellent__
3–Well Below Average	Arm Accuracy		5	6	Knuckle Ball				Emot. Maturity __good__
2–Poor	Fielding	*	7	5	Other	*			Married __no__
	Range		4	5	Poise				
Use One Grade	Baseball Instinct		4	5	Baseball Instinct				Date Eligible
Grade On Major	Aggressiveness		6	6	Aggressiveness				__06-79__
League Standards	Pull	Str. Away	Opp. Field		Arm Action _____				Phase
Not Amateur	__X__	_____	_____		Delivery _____				__Reg__

Physical Description (Injuries, Glasses, etc.) GRADUATION __06-79__

TALL, WELL PROP. STRONG BUILD, ATHLETIC BODY.

Abilities

SOUND HITTING MECH., good BAT SPEED & LEVERAGE. CONSISTANT CONTACT, CAN DRIVE BALL. AB. Ave. ARM STRENGTH. Ave. RUNNER. FAIR RECEIVER WITH POT. TO IMPROVE. Agg. PLAYER.

Weaknesses

LONG POWER STROKE, STARTS SWING WITH STIFF FRONT ARM, BUT IS STRONG ENUF TO GET BAT OUT IN FRONT.

TAKES TOO LONG GETTING RID OF BALL, WINDS UP A LITTLE.

Summation and Signability Worth _____

RAISE OFF. 6 PTS. HAS TOOLS TO BE FRONT LINE PLAYER. LIKE HIS ENTHUSIASM. NEEDS SOME REFINEMENT BEHIND PLATE.

Jay Schroeder always wanted to play baseball. As a high school kid in California he was so good that the Toronto Blue Jays drafted him as their first pick in the June 1979 draft. He played in their organization while he went to U.C.L.A. and played football. In the minors, Schroeder was converted into an outfielder and tried playing third base, but he wasn't comfortable at those positions. He considered himself a catcher and actually liked playing that terrifying position. In four minor league seasons Schroeder failed to post impressive numbers. When the Washington Redskins drafted him in 1984, he hung up his mitt and mask and went into the NFL. At Washington he was Joe Theismann's understudy and was pressed into action when the veteran quarterback was injured in a game in November 1985. Schroeder was spectacular for the rest of the season and had a great 1986 when he shared the NFL lead for completions with 276. After a disappointing season in 1987, Schroeder was traded to the Oakland Raiders early in 1988.

■ ■ ■

It would seem that if you're a two-sport man, you have to choose one and stick with it. Usually, but not always. The exception is Deion Sanders. He does both and, more importantly, he does both well. Sanders was drafted by the Kansas City Royals in the sixth round of the 1985 draft when he had finished high school. But Sanders chose to go to Florida State on a football scholarship where he won national honors as a defensive back for three years. The Yankees, who obviously had been burned in the John Elway affair and who had become a bit uneasy about signing football players, drafted Sanders in the thirtieth round in 1988. He played that year for three Yankee minor league teams without showing too much. In the 1989 NFL draft, Sanders was picked as the Falcons' first choice. He signed with the Atlanta eleven in September and played that season at cornerback. Sanders had no intention of giving up either baseball for football or football for baseball. He would work at both. This made the Yankees very uncomfortable. Their prospect was risking injuries that could make a return on their investment zip. Besides, Sanders had a bit too much flash for the Yankees' taste, so after two short visits to the majors, Sanders was traded to the Atlanta Braves.

With the Braves, Sanders started to fulfill his baseball potential. He hit .304 in 1992 and led the NL with 14 triples before hitting .533 in the four-game World Series. After that he put on the pads and went on to lead the NFL in kickoff return yardage with 1,067. Sanders's contract with the Falcons stipulated that he could finish out the baseball season before he had to report for football. From 1991 through 1993, Braves and Falcons fans were able to watch him perform in the spring, summer, fall, and winter, making Deion Sanders Atlanta's man for all seasons. That ended in 1994, when the Braves traded him to the Cincinnati Reds and he left the Falcons to play football with the San Francisco 49ers.

KANSAS CITY ROYALS
FREE AGENT REPORT

OFFICE USE
Report No. _____
Player No. _____

Overall Future Potential ___64___

Nat'l. Double Check Yes ✓ No_____

Scout's Report # ___1___   Scout _TOM FERRICK_

PLAYER ___SANDERS DION___ Pos. _CF_ Date _____
　　　Last Name　　First Name　Middle Initial

School or Team ___N. FT. MYERS___ City and State _____

Permanent Address _____
　　　Street　　City　　St　　Zip　　Phone

Current Address _____
　　　Street　　City　　St　　Zip　　Phone

Date of Birth _8|9|67_ Ht. _6'2"_ Wt. _170_ Bats _L_ Throws _L_ DATE ELIGIBLE _JUNE 85_ PHASE _R_

Game Date(s) _4/1/85 4/5/85_ Games ___2___ Innings ___11___ Graduation _JUNE '85_

No.	RATING KEY	M.P.H.	NON-PITCHERS	Pres.	Fut.	PITCHERS	Pres.	Fut.	MAKEUP					
8—Outstanding		94-	Hitting Ability	4	6	Fast Ball					Ex.	Good	Fair	Poor
7—Very Good		91-93	Power	5	6	Life of Fastball								
6—Above Average		88-90	Running Speed	7	7	Curve			Habits		4	✓3	2	1
5—Average		85-87	Base Running	4	6	Control			Dedication		4	✓3	2	1
4—Below Average		82-84	Arm Strength	4	4	Change of Pace			Agility		✓4	3	2	1
3—Well Below Ave.		79-81	Arm Accuracy	4	5	Slider			Aptitude		4	✓3	2	1
2—Poor		0-78	Fielding	4	6	Other			Phys. Mat.		4	✓3	2	1
			Range	5	6	Poise			Emot. Mat.		4	✓3	2	1

USE ONE GRADE	Hitting: (√)	Running						Baseball Inst.	✓4	3	2	1
Grade On	Pull ......3 ✓	Time To		EX	GOOD	FAIR	POOR	Aggressive-	✓4	3	2	1
Major League	St. Away ....2 ___	1st Base			Arm Action	4	3	2	1	ness			
Standard	Opp. Field..1 ___					3/4	OH	SIDE	OTHER	OVERALL	4	✓3	2	1
		4.0		Delivery	4	3	2	1					
				Gun Reading ___ to ___ MPH								

Physical Description (Injuries, Glasses, etc.) NO GLASSES. TALL- RANGY - LONG LEGGED GOOD FOREARMS. GROWING ROOM. BUILT LIKE JERRY MUMPHRLEY (ASTROS). BASKETBALL - BASEBALL + FOOTBALL (QB) ALL AROUND ATHLETE

Abilities AGILITY- QUICKNESS ON 1ST STEP. SURE HANDED +RANGE GOOD IN OF. GOOD INSTINCTS IN STEALING BASES. BAT SPEED GOOD. SHOWS SOME ARM STRENGTH. SHOULD BE ABOVE AVERAGE DEF. OF. POWER TO ALL FIELDS. OF OR 1B.

Weaknesses ARM + NOW HAS SLIGHT HAND HITCH IN BAT MECHANICS. CAN BE CORRECTED. LUNGES ON CURVE. CORRECT ABLE. HAS RANGE FOR CF BUT DEFINITE L.F. ARM. THROWING AND MECHANICS NEED HELP.

Signability: Ex._____ Good ✓ Fair _____ Poor_____ Worth: $ _45,000_
SIGNED LETTER OF INTENT TO FLA. STATE. (FOOTBALL QB + ALSO BASEBALL. (WON'T BE ALLOWED TO PLAY BASEBALL IN 1ST YEAR AT FLA.ST.) 2.5 ACADEMIC AVERAGE. WANTS TO PLAY BASEBALL.

Makeup Evaluation and Player Summation ALL AROUND ATHLETE. MISSED FIRST FIVE GAMES BECAUSE OF BASKETBALL. BOY INDICATED HE WANTS BASEBALL NOW.

FEIRRICK

MAY   1967

Physical Description: 6:00 - 190 · STURDY ATH-
LONG ARM
MMER
OUND.
· FLEXIBL

PROSPE

NE   VIDA
(ams)   (First Na

Action

DESOTO
ETHUNE H
MANSFIE
(City)
REGULAR

2 FBS
FBS
) GOOD
GOOD.
ING FBS
LE ARM
MO &
OWS SOM
OVE TO 2
(ODDLY ENOUGH) BETTER TO 1B. FINE ARM

☑ Suggest
eligible t
☐ Suggest we look at him again.
☐ Suggest his file be closed.

mended for signing, fill in the following:

nite ML prospect ✓   Date Eligible to Sign   JUNE 1967
ge ML Prospect   Number games seen
t in class ROOKIE   to date   1
Stop Watch Time to First Base

Weaknesses: OVER SLIDES IN DELIVERIN
BALL. REAL LONG STRIDE. LANDS
ON LEFT HEEL. CURVE FLAT. NEED
HELP IN MOST PHASES OF PITCHING
STARTING WITH DELIVERY FIRST.
SLOW MOVING BUT CAN RUN.

KEY		Present	Future	PITCHERS	Present	Future
Major andards— ar.	Hitting Ability			Fast Ball	3	2
	Power			Curve	4	3
	Base running			Control	4	3
g	Arm (strength)			Change of Pace	NONE	
Av.	Arm (accuracy)			Slider	NONE	
	Field			Other Pitches	NONE	
	Range			Field	4	3
	Baseball Instinct			Baseball Instinct	4	3

Av.   Pull __ Straight Away __ Opposite Field __
Habits   Habits   GOOD
Aggressive   Aggressive   FAIR

Summation and other comments including any information that
may have bearing on his signing or not signing at this time.

HAS MAJOR LEAGUE ARM & BODY.
SHOW 2 VELOCITY QUITE OFTEN
DESPITE BAD DELIVERY. MAJOR
LEAGUE PROSPECT. C STUDENT
FATHER DEAD. OLDEST OF 6 CHILDREN
WILL TAKE COLLEGE PLUS $15,000 OR $20,000
GRAMBLING COLLEGE INTERESTED IN BOY.

What should we offer:

py to Director of Scouting. Keep white copy for your file.

MEL DIDIER

ON THE DOTTED LINE

Mel Didier has been a scout for the Montreal Expos, the Atlanta Braves, and the Los Angeles Dodgers. He is strictly a bottom-line man. When he finds a prospect who fits the club's needs, he's only done half the job. Signing the youngster completes it. Mel is a great closer, and three stories illustrate how proficient he is. In 1967 Ralph Garr was a star second baseman at Grambling. He had an astounding .582 batting average, and the Atlanta Braves made him their number three draft pick that year. Paul Richards was in charge of signing players for Atlanta and assigned Mel to get the youngster. Mel spoke to Garr, who told Mel that he had retained a lawyer to represent him in the negotiations. When Richards heard about Garr's representation, he fumed, then exploded. "We don't negotiate with agents or lawyers. Forget it," he told Didier.

Richards was an old-time baseball man who learned the business of baseball in an era when the players were looked upon by the clubs as chattel. There were no lawyers or agents to trouble the deal in the "Good Old Days." The fact that the clubs had lawyers on staff to "fine print" their contracts while the players went unrepresented didn't strike Richards as anything but natural. "This is baseball," he believed, "not a business." How's that for around the bases? Feudalism to naivete to gall. But Mel knew that Garr had a talent that one sees rarely. He also knew that Ralph could stay in Grambling for his senior year and go back into the draft in 1968, which would invalidate the Braves' claim on him. Didier couldn't allow this to happen. This twenty-one-year-old hit over .500 as a junior. Maybe as a senior he might not make out at all! Mel sighted Garr in his cross-hairs and went to work.

Garr's lawyer wanted $100,000 for signing, which was way beyond what the Braves were prepared to pay, so there was no sense talking to him. Mel went to Garr directly. Obviously the youngster wasn't told that he should let his lawyer do all the talking, and Mel is a persuasive guy. He told Garr that the Braves' offer was a good one for a third-round draft choice; $20,000 plus an incentive bonus of $7,500, and they would pay for his last year in Grambling. It was a package worth a total of $30,000. Keep remembering that this was in 1967, about a light year and a half away from the economics of today with its astronomical numbers.

When Garr, with visions of megabucks dancing in his head, said that this wasn't anywhere near what his lawyer said he was worth, Didier asked him what his lawyer said about Garr's fielding at second base? There wasn't $100,000 worth of talent on display when Garr played infield. Garr started to bend, and then he made a counteroffer to Didier. "I'll go for the deal plus a new car." Didier could taste the ink on the contract. Okay, he would try to get Garr a nice, new car. "A Cadillac," said Ralph in parting. When Mel told Richards about the money part of the deal, Richards was happy. It didn't last long. When Didier mentioned the Cadillac, Richards had this helpful bit of negotiating strategy for Mel, "Tell the kid to go to hell."

Back to Garr with the bad news went Didier. No car. Then Garr reopened the negotiations. "I'll settle for a Chevy." Back went Mel to Richards with the good news. "My last offer still stands," Richards snapped, "the kid can go to hell." Didier told Garr that the offer of $30,000 was final; take it or leave it. But Garr wanted to give it one more shot. "Make it a pickup truck," he told Mel. That didn't make things a lot better. Didier realized that it was a matter of principle with Richards and that principle was making his boss foolish. He risked losing Garr for a modest consideration. Also, it was now becoming a matter of principle with Garr. Mel had to solve this dilemma, so he phoned Richards and said that he would buy the kid the pickup himself to clinch the deal.

Richards didn't say anything, and the silence told Didier that he had won. Mel started fantasizing about riding down Peach Tree Street in a World Series parade happily waving to the crowds while sitting next to Garr in the pickup truck. Richards interrupted Mel's reverie, "We'll buy the truck," he said abruptly and hung up. Ralph Garr was now a Brave. "He had stiff hands at second base so we switched him to the outfield," Didier said. There Garr played thirteen years and had a lifetime BA of .306. In 1974 Garr led the NL with a .353 BA, 214 hits, and 17 triples. One wonders if Ralph still has the truck.

While researching the Braves' draft choices in 1967, you come upon a name of a player who was selected immediately after Garr. The name jumps out at you. "What about the kid who was the number-four draft choice for the Braves in 1967?" I asked Mel. He laughed, "Let me tell you about that," Mel said. "I was coaching baseball at L.S.U. while I was scouting for the Braves. One day I get a call from the Atlanta scouting director saying that Paul Richards and John

McHale were wondering why had I made a report on every good-looking prospect in Louisiana and not on a hot high school catcher who was being scouted by other teams. I didn't know who they were talking about. 'You should know. He's living in your house,' Richards said, kind of angry. Bob Didier is my son. But I didn't know other teams were scouting him. They never told either Bob or me. I didn't want to put in a report on Bob. I wanted him to be seen by impartial judges, so Jim Fanning and Ray Hayworth, two good former major league catchers who were working for the Braves, came down and saw Bob. They liked him and the Braves put him on their draft list. He came to us in the fourth round."

Now Mel was faced with a classic conflict of interest. He was both the player's father and the guy who signed prospects. In effect, he was both sides in the deal. In order to avoid negotitations which could be embarrassing and also avoid becoming totally schizoid, Mel made the same deal for Bob as the Braves had made for Ralph Garr, with two exceptions. Under Bob's contract, he was to take spring training with the Braves for two years, even though he might be on a minor league roster. It guaranteed that Bob would be seen by the Atlanta brass instead of possibly being buried in the minors. The Braves agreed. The other exception was that Bob Didier never got a pickup truck. He played in the majors for six years and was on the Braves' 1969 NL West Championship team.

"You know about Andre Dawson?" Mel asked, and he was off and running. "It was while I was a scout with the Montreal Expos. We had drafted a third baseman named Randy Eickenhorst from Gulf Coast Junior College and I went down to see him. We weren't going to sign him until the school season ended. That day his team was playing Florida A&M and Dawson was the A&M shortstop. I liked his arm. Then he went out to play center field, and he was even more impressive. I said to myself, I want this kid. But you have to play it cool. You never want to show your interest in a player because other scouts find out about it fast. I looked for the A&M kid furthest down on the team's totem pole to talk to—the equipment manager. I asked him about two other ballplayers I had no interest in, and then I said, 'How about that kid in center field?' He told me that Andre was listed as a sophomore, but he really was a junior. He had hurt his knee playing football, so he had one more year of football eligibility than he did in baseball. I couldn't believe my luck. Since Dawson was a bona fide junior that meant we could draft him. He had a bat as quick as Hank Aaron's.

"I invited Andre to a tryout clinic I was conducting, and he showed good speed. When he took his turn at bat, he hit the first pitch, a bullet, right back at the pitcher. It hit the poor kid in the knee and he had to be carried off the field. The next pitch Andre hit off the wall in left field and the next one off the wall in straight away center. I went up to him in the batting cage and said, 'Get out of there,' because I didn't want anyone to become too interested. In 1975 the Expos needed a lot of new players in the organization. In that year's draft we took as many kids as we could and hoped that no one would pick Dawson. Our luck held out, and we selected him in the eleventh round. We took a real chance; it was stupid to wait that long. I signed Andre for a $2,500 bonus."

To this day, Dawson and Didier are close friends. "He's one of the greatest human beings that ever walked," Mel says flat out. Dawson's nineteen excellent years in the majors, including a league-leading 49 home runs and 137 RBIs in 1987, have justified Didier's confidence in Dawson's greatness.

But $2,500? If any of you out there have some refrigerators you want to get rid of, give Mel Didier a few catalogs and a map of the Aleutians and your worries are over.

GEORGE DIGBY

THAT'S WHAT I LIKE ABOUT THE SOUTH

George Digby is a Southern gentleman who has scouted the South for the Boston Red Sox for over fifty years. When you talk to George, he escorts you back to a more interesting time in America. He talks about train travel. "In the old days, you could cover your area by train. Trains went everywhere. You could take the Southern Pacific out of New Orleans or the Southern Atlantic up to Athens, Georgia, or Atlanta. You could do your paperwork in comfort. And at every railroad stop, there was a nice railroad hotel you could stay at."

George was an area scout until a few years ago, when he became a "cross-checker." Now he reviews the reports sent to him by area scouts and then takes a look at the prospects that he feels are most promising. "You're not going to be right all the time," Digby says philosophically. Yet when asked for some of the name players he missed, he'd rather not discuss the subject. The ones he's signed and became major leaguers should be more interesting to a listener, George figures. He's right.

George points with justifiable pride to Wade Boggs, the great third baseman now with the Yankees, who has led the league in hitting four times and has a lifetime BA of over .330. "We got him in the 1976 draft and I signed him for a $7,500 bonus." Digby claims that when Boggs was in high school in Tampa, Florida, he didn't attract as much attention as one might think. He wasn't a good fielder. That accounts for his being overlooked in the first six rounds by every team. He was pick number seven for the Red Sox. What did George see in Boggs that others didn't? "I'm a bat man," George says. "I like aggressiveness at the plate. If a kid has good bat speed, I don't worry too much about his fielding. Good hitting makes up for a lot of errors." As a dedicated "bat man," George wishes there had been the designated hitter earlier. "I could have signed a lot of kids who could really hit but who were poor in the field," Digby laments.

How does George go about signing a prospect? "Before the 1965 draft you had to wait until a boy graduated high school, or until his class graduated high school. Then I would contact him and tell him the Red Sox story. There were a lot of Ted Williams fans down South, and a lot of the kids saw themselves playing in the same outfield with Ted." Of course, this was as close to being a fantasy as squaring the circle because guys like Dom DiMaggio, Jackie Jensen, and Jimmy Piersall were playing alongside Williams. But hope springs eternal, and George was a salesman. And in those days he didn't have to worry about losing his prospect to another team in a draft.

"The secret of scouting is don't prejudge a youngster. Make him make you like him. And don't be rattled if the kid has a bad day. Check out his fundamentals," George advises.

The money that ballplayers get today seems so outrageous to Digby that he can't seem to grasp the new economic realities. "We have a kid who we drafted and wanted to sign. Trot Nixon. His father is a doctor who invented the kidney machine, so he's a multimillionaire. We offered the kid $600,000 and thought we had a deal. Just as we were about to sign him, on the last possible day, he asked for $700,000. If you don't sign your first draft choice, the club doesn't like it. We managed to give him what he asked for." Perhaps George thought that the kid already had so much money that he wouldn't want more. Unfortunately, it doesn't work that way. In 1994, Trot Nixon played at Lynchburg of the Carolina League where a lot of people in the Red Sox organization were watching their investment very closely.

Digby loves scouting in the South. "Kids here play ball twelve months out of the year. In 1982 in Florida we had three number one draft choices from high school teams. The Mets took Dwight Gooden, who pitched for Hillsborough High in Tampa, the Tigers took Rich Monteleone, who pitched for Catholic High, also in Tampa, and the White Sox took Ron Karkovice, who was a catcher for Boone High in Orlando." George's voice almost coos with Southern pride.

TOM FERRICK

CHARACTER COUNTS

"It takes four or five years to learn how to scout," says Tom Ferrick, who's been scouting for Kansas City since 1965. "You have to learn what to look for." This from a man who was a major leaguer for nine years and a pitching coach for twelve. In other words, with over twenty years of experience, it still took time to know how to judge a prospect. "Projecting how a youngster will do. That's the tough part. His physical ability is obvious." Tom has great respect for the intangibles of the game, and they start with "character."

Without any hint of zealotry, Ferrick has a strong sense of morality. He has seen too many great prospects and professionals damage or destroy their careers by high living and reckless behavior off the field. Ferrick cites as an example Mickey Mantle. When Mantle came to New York City, the Yankees foolishly roomed him with two veterans in an apartment over the Stage Delicatessen in the heart of The Great White Way. Thirty-five-year-old Johnny Hopp and twenty-nine-year-old Hank Bauer knew where the action was, and they introduced the nineteen-year-old kid from Commerce, Oklahoma, to the bright lights and the spectacular temptations of Broadway. One had to be more of a saint than Mantle was to resist such goodies. As a result, Mantle hit a disappointing .267 in 96 games as a rookie, and people started to wonder about this well-publicized superhero.

When Ferrick is interested in a prospect, he likes to spend time with the youngster and with the youngster's parents. "You can get the feel for a kid's makeup by talking to the family. Physical ability is one thing, but character and habits are just as important."

Ferrick feels that scouting is one of the most difficult jobs in baseball. "You go out to see a kid in a high school game and you never know what you're liable to see. Some high school games are pitiful. A guy can look like a standout playing against poor competition, but how will he be playing against better kids?" Ferrick asks. Often a scout must make his projection on very little information, using a lot of guesswork. But what's the alternative? There isn't any, Ferrick feels. "You could become negative and say no 95 percent of the time and know that you'll be right. After all, only about 5 or 6 percent of all the kids drafted make the big leagues. But you won't have any players."

Tom's opinion on the value of the Major League Scouting Bureau differs from Lenny Merullo's. Tom says the Bureau started when the owners became aware that twenty or more scouts were watching the same top prospects. So they felt they could save money by having a central scouting bureau, thereby eliminating the need for so many team scouts. Says Ferrick, "It doesn't make sense because it doesn't save any money. No matter what the Bureau scout says, the club must send their own man to check out the report. So why do the clubs spend $100,000 a year to operate the bureau?" Tom didn't know the answer to that one. He'd much rather see the money go toward paying the scouts a decent salary.

"A scout is anonymous," Tom said. "He doesn't get credit for what he's accomplished, and the clubs like to keep it that way. For years Birdie Tebbetts has been trying to get someone at the Hall of Fame Museum to put up a plaque or something with some scouts' names on it, but he's given up trying. It's not a lot to ask. They should recognize scouts like Yankee scout Paul Kritchel, who discovered Lou Gehrig and Whitey Ford, or Washington's Joe Cambria, who scouted all those Latin Americans for the Senators and signed Camilo Pascual, or Howie Haak, who signed, among many others, Roberto Clemente." Incidentally, Joe Cambria once scouted a prospect who, had he not been turned down, might have changed the course of twentieth-century history. The prospect's name was Fidel Castro.

Tom Ferrick continues to hope and wait for simple decency, if not justice, for the scouts from the people who run baseball. He will have a long wait. As of this writing there is nothing at the Hall of Fame Museum that mentions baseball scouts, and there are no plans to do so in the near future.

TOM GIORDANO

PAST, PRESENT, AND FUTURE

Cleveland Indian scout Tom Giordano has been scouting for thirty-five years and has been in professional baseball for fifty. As a player he put in twelve years in the minors and, as he says, "had a cup of coffee" with the Philadelphia Athletics in September 1953. He was brought up after his season with Savannah in the Sally League ended. At Savannah that year, Tom proudly recalls, he led the league with 24 home runs. That was two more than the runner-up for homer honors, a player named Hank Aaron. In Tom's second at-bat with the Athletics, he got his first major league hit, a home run. One can sense the pride that lives behind Tom's natural, graceful modesty. But his quiet .175 batting average and the fact that he was a twenty-eight-year-old rookie did not impress the A's. They gave up on him and sent him back down to Triple A ball at Ottawa. In 1955 he called it quits and decided to become a minor league manager. He managed at Leesburg in the Florida State League and then at Selma in the Alabama Florida League.

In 1960, Tom quit managing and took up scouting. At the time he was a Phys. Ed. teacher in Copiague High School on Long Island. Scouting, being seasonal work in the Northeast, meant that Tom could keep his teaching position and also scout when school was out in the summer. In 1976 Tom became scouting director for the Baltimore Orioles, where he stayed until 1987. Tom went to Cleveland in 1988, and for two years he was the vice president of baseball operations. Desiring to taper off in his activities—Tom was then sixty-five—he became a major

177

league scout. A major league scout is one who scouts only the players who are already in the majors or high minors. Tom's reports furnish the information the Cleveland Indians need to formulate their plans for trades. For someone who was tapering off, Tom has a lot on his plate. He scouts the Yankees, Phillies, Mets, Red Sox, Toronto, and Montreal and their Triple A and Double A affiliates. That way the Indians know the depth of each team and the players who might become available. When a deal is possible between the Indians and another club, the front office dispatches Tom to size up the player or players involved. He will call on the general manager of the club, tell him why he's there, follow the player for six or seven games, and make his report. "The most important thing," Giordano emphasizes, "is a scout's gut feeling.

"Regular scouting today is totally different from what it was before 1965 because of the free agent draft. Before the draft a scout ran his own territory and when he zeroed in on a player, he attached himself to the family. When they wanted to get down to business, the family wanted to do business with that scout. He sold himself to the family." Now after a scout recognizes a talent, he turns the prospect's name over to the front office and the club takes over. They use what is known as "the cross-check system." The final decisions on which prospects to draft are made by the scouting director, his supervisors, and the national cross-checker, who has reviewed the area scouts' and regional cross-checkers' reports.

Although Tom was once the Major League Scouting Bureau director, he is not an advocate of the central system. He prefers the old method when the scout would go out, find the talent, and then sign him instead of sharing the information with all the clubs. He thinks that most of the team scouts and even the clubs themselves feel the same way. Tom poses an interesting question. "If a team's scout saw a player who he liked but the scout from the ML Bureau didn't or the other way around, who would the club listen to?" The implication is clear; there's one scout too many.

Talking to an "old timer" like Tom Giordano, one would not expect him to say that today's prospects are better ballplayers than the prospects of twenty years ago. But that's what he maintains: "Youngsters today are stronger because of proper nutrition and conditioning." However, there is a down side, Tom believes. "In 1993 there were 105 major league players on the DL at one time. I have to believe this is due to the misuse of training regimens and especially weight programs."

Asked how he feels when a prospect fails to live up to his high expectations, Tom responds with a story about a youngster from New York City named Dallas Williams. Some scouts had learned about Williams's talent when he was only fourteen years old and had watched him through high school. The Orioles drafted and signed Williams. Giordano said, "He had all the tools, and I figured he had immense potential." But Tom was wrong. The unfortunate fact was that Williams didn't have potential. What was there when he was eighteen was all there was or ever would be. Tom said, "I felt bad. He was my first number one. He had a cup of coffee in the big leagues [as did some other player he talked about earlier] and never made it. It hurts when something like that happens."

Tom Giordano is a special man. His uniqueness and character are illustrated by the story he tells about his very close friend, the late Dodger scout Reggie Otero. On the eve of the 1976 June draft, Reggie called Tom and asked what he thought of a high school catcher named Mike Scioscia. "Reggie and I were close friends, so I leveled with him and told him that Scioscia was a real talent and that we wanted him as our first pick. That year the Dodgers had the nineteenth pick and we had the twentieth and I asked him not to make me look silly. He said he wouldn't and the next day, as I was holding the card that said, 'Scioscia' in my hand, the Dodger spokesman announced that they were picking Mike as their first choice. I was really taken aback. Maybe I shouldn't have told him how we felt about Scioscia, but he was my friend and you don't lie to friends." Reggie was properly embarrassed by his betrayal, but Tom maintained his affection for Reggie until the latter passed away. That's the kind of guy Tom Giordano is. And by the way, the player the Orioles chose to replace Scioscia as their first choice was Dallas Williams. Tom didn't mention this.

Where does Tom feel that baseball is headed? He is not too optimistic. "Every day we get people with nonbaseball backgrounds taking over positions of authority. They don't listen to veterans who know the game. Also in scouting we are getting more people who do not have a solid baseball background. A lot of us old guys spent time as players or coaches or managers. Today's younger scouting directors haven't had that kind of experience. But the younger people in the front office choose them because they feel more comfortable with their contemporaries than they do with seasoned veterans. The old timer, even though he may have many productive years ahead of him, is shoved aside for these younger guys who seem to be making most of the decisions. Corporate America has taken over the front office."

Tom feels that scouts are always underrated, if not totally overlooked, by the baseball community. He would like to see some recognition for the vital part they play by according them a section in the Hall of Fame. "If they have room for broadcasters in Cooperstown, why not for scouts?" Among his candidates for recognition are scouts like Tom Greenwade, Howie Haak, Hugh Alexander, and Turk Karem. Typically modest, he didn't mention Tom Giordano.

HOWIE HAAK

A Half Century on the Road

"You gotta talk to Howie Haak." I kept hearing this every time I spoke to a scout. "Howie knows everyone and everything about baseball. He's got great stories." One seldom hears of anyone who is as respected and admired by his colleagues as much as Howie. When I called him in California, he didn't sound like the upbeat, garrulous person I had expected; he sounded down. He told me that he had just been let go by Houston after having been a scout for forty-eight years. Obviously he hadn't won the respect and admiration of the Astro management.

"I'm eighty-two years old and I don't know what the hell I'm going to do. When I don't have baseball, all I have is television and sleep." If you really want sadistic satisfaction from being cruel, try it on the elderly or the infirm. "They don't want guys like me. It's about insurance. They're afraid that I'd get cancer and need a lot of treatment. The only old guys they want are the ones who'll take $7,500 to add to their Social Security. They don't want to pay me what I was getting." I didn't ask if Howie would accept the Social Security deal. I knew better.

Howie Haak started in baseball in the Cardinal farm system and played from 1931 until he hurt his arm in 1937. After that he worked for Branch Rickey in the St. Louis organization as a coach and traveling secretary for four years. In 1941 Haak went into the Navy and after the war rejoined Rickey who had moved to the Brooklyn Dodgers. There, Howie became a scout. In 1951 when Rickey moved again, this time to Pittsburgh, Howie followed. Rickey sent Howie to Latin

America to scout in the Dominican Republic, Puerto Rico, Venezuela, and Panama, areas with a large, untapped talent pool. Up to that time only Joe Cambria, a scout for the Washington Senators, had worked south of the border. Cambria only scouted in Cuba, leaving a huge area for Howie.

Haak signed many of the important Latin players who played with the Pirates from the mid-'50s until the '90s. But his "chef d'oeuvre" was his signing of Roberto Clemente. The Dodger had signed Clemente as a bonus player and had sent him to Montreal, then in the International League. There he was used very sparingly, but Branch Rickey knew about Clemente and sent Haak to Montreal to scout him in August 1954. The Dodgers were trying to hide Clemente because he would come up for the draft, as it was then structured, the following season. The Dodgers weren't about to advertise his talents.

Haak watched as Montreal only used him in four games in the last few weeks of the season. "They had him batting seventh," Haak chuckled. "In the final game there were men on base and they pinch hit for Clemente." Haak saw Clemente after the game and the future Hall of Famer was livid. "He was going to jump the club, but if he did that he would be declared ineligible for a year and then be put back into the draft the year he was reinstated. Pittsburgh had finished last in '54, so we had the first pick in the '55 draft. We could get him, but if he had to be out a year and then got back into the regular draft, we would probably have lost him. So I convinced Clemente not to jump and promised him that if he came with us, he would be playing in Pittsburgh in '55. We got him in the draft for $4,000. From then on, I had Latin America as my territory and I didn't even speak Spanish."

Howie readily admits to missing a few. "There's one kid I could have signed but I didn't. I could have had him for $300—Juan Marichal," Howie said with resignation born of decades of experience. "Marichal was only fifteen or sixteen years old at the time, about 5'10" and weighed about 140 pounds. He couldn't blacken your eye. All he had was that big kick and a soft curve. The Giants signed him the next year and didn't even take him to spring training, didn't pay his salary, and kept him home. Then the next year he came out and won 20 games in Michigan, then he went to Springfield and won, and then he went to Phoenix for half a year and then the Giants brought him up." Juan Marichal became one of the greatest pitchers of the 1960s. He won twenty or more games and had over 200 strikeouts a season six times. He was inducted into the Hall of Fame in 1983.

When asked, Howie dismissed the ones he missed with a verbal shrug. "That's the way it goes." But his next stories contradicted his seeming detachment. "I had one kid that got himself killed. His name was Emead and I gave him $17,000 and he went right into Class B. No Rookie League or Class C. He was hitting .331 with 31 doubles, 17 triples, and seven home runs. He dove for a ball and hit the second baseman. He died right on the field. The medical examiner said that he had a rare thin skull condition and that any hard concussion could have killed him. Nobody knew about that, not the kid or his family." The fact that Howie remembers Emead's numbers all these years tells you something.

Gino Cimoli was Haak's most difficult signing. As Howie tells it, "In 1948 San Francisco offered him $8,000 to sign. His mother wanted him to play in San Francisco because they wouldn't send him out. It was also where the family lived, and Gino was only a little over eighteen. I was offering $12,000 to go with Brooklyn. His father wanted him to go with Brooklyn and so did Gino. I used to go over to their house at eight o'clock in the morning and stay until four in the afternoon and drive his father to work. Then I'd take Gino to a show and eat dinner and I'd come back to the house, drop off the kid and wait outside in my car until the last scout's car left, which could be two-thirty in the morning.

"I did it for four days and I called Rickey and I told him 'Jesus, I'm not going to be able to sign this guy.' He asked me if I could strengthen the father's backbone, and I said I'd try but don't get upset when you get the liquor bill. One night we were drinking coffee royales, I asked the guy, 'Who wears the pants in this family?' He got pissed and said that he did. Then I asked him why, if he wanted his kid to go with Brooklyn and we were offering him $4,000 more, why the hell doesn't he sign with us? He said, 'We'll sign. Right now.' He woke up his wife and they signed in the middle of the night." Cimoli went on to have a ten-year major league career.

On the subject of traveling, Haak offers the following: "I once had to see a pitcher in Rochester, New York, and I'm out here in California. I fly there and I get a mile from the ballpark and it rains like a sonofabitch. I get on a plane and go to Portland, Oregon, the next day to see Wally Backman and I get rained out there. Now I get back on the plane and go back to Rochester for a game on Friday and I get rained out there. So I went back and forth across the country four times and I didn't see anyone."

Howie Haak has given the game over a half century of exceptional service, and he remembers it all with great warmth. It would be fitting for the people who run baseball to show some warmth to Howie Haak. But that's baseball.

AL KUBSKI

You Need A Crystal Ball

Al Kubski used to be an area scout for Baltimore and Kansas City before his wife's illness made him cut down on his activities. He is now a cross-checker for the Royals. "I cover Southern California, but that's still a lot of ground," Al said. One senses that he would rather talk baseball than discuss his personal ups and downs, so we spoke about pitching and about drugs. First pitching. Al talked about Dan Quisenberry, who was a superb relief pitcher for the Royals for nine of his twelve big-league seasons. Quiz led the AL in saves in 1980 and from 1982 through 1985. Quiz ranks number seven in the majors in lifetime saves with a total of 244.

"Quiz wasn't drafted when he became eligible," Al said. "But a lot of guys never were." The list includes Bobby Bonilla, Kevin Mitchell, and Larry Bowa. "Quiz was at LeMoyne Junior College in California and he asked his hitting coach Ben Heinz to call Royals' scout Rosie Gilhousen to see if K.C. needed what we call an organization player. That's a player who'll never be a star but can give you a dependable performance. Rosie was leaving to see a high school tournament in Arizona, and Quiz offered to drive down to Rosie's home about 125 miles away and talk to him. He did and Rosie signed Quiz for a $500-a-month-salary. He just wanted a chance to play." Quiz was the kind of pitcher you would let play catch in your backyard because if he threw one wild, it wouldn't break any windows.

"His fastball was nothing," Al said, "Maybe eighty miles an hour if that. When he was in the minors a bullpen catcher told Quiz that he would never make it with that kind of speed. He should try something different and suggested that he try pitching underneath. Quiz did and he had a great career and he became a millionaire by using that confusing delivery.

"Many years later Quiz asked me how come I never tried to sign him. I kidded him. I said, 'I saw you pitch in high school, I saw you pitch in junior college, and I saw you pitch tonight with the Royals, and I still don't think you have anything.' He laughed. He was still pitching 78 mph as a major leaguer; but they couldn't hit his junk." Quisenberry's lifetime ERA of 2.76 attests to this.

"You like to see kids who can pitch 90 mph. But quite often somebody'll get guys out and you ask yourself, 'What's he got?' Frank Tanana had a 78 mph fastball for the last four years he was in the majors. But he knew how to pitch. Guys like Stu Miller and Eddie Lopat were famous for having nothing. Yet they won. Jackie Robinson once said of Jim Konstanty, the Phillies' reliever, 'I don't know why we can't hit that guy.' But Konstanty had a deceptive motion that kept the batters off balance and popping up. Today we don't give a youngster a chance to learn how to pitch.

"Know about Saberhagen?" Al asked. "He was a pitcher and shortstop in high school in the San Fernando Valley near L.A. He was a skinny kid. He weighed only 160 pounds. K.C. scout Guy Hansen saw him play and liked him. But there was word that Brett had hurt his arm by playing every game instead of resting between the games he pitched. If a pitcher is a good athlete, a lot of high school coaches will play him all the time. They shouldn't. It's not fair to the kid. Anyway, Guy put Brett's name in for the draft as our nineteenth pick and we got him. After the season Saberhagen pitches in a city championship game at Dodger Stadium and pitches a no-hitter and almost a perfect game except for an error that allowed a runner. He wasn't fast, only 84 mph, where the average is 87 or so. But he had a good delivery, threw strikes, and didn't walk anybody. He was very impressive. Now, after the game college offers started coming in. Up to then he was all set to sign with us for a $5,000 bonus. But now, his father suddenly had a star and wanted more. It got real nasty because we had the rights to Brett. We finally agreed and signed him for $20,000. He won the Cy Young Award twice with K.C." Al said that over the years Saberhagen bulked up to 190 pounds and his fastball now is clocked at 92 mph. Kubski added disapprovingly, "But he runs around too much in New York." He made it sound like the Big Apple was the only city in which you could get in trouble.

"I tried to get the Orioles to get Tom Seaver when I was with Baltimore," Al said. "The Orioles wanted to give him $12,000. He wanted more, and he was right." Kubiski saw Seaver pitch against an all-pro team in an exhibition, and he was terrific. Later, after that draft business, he was in Jacksonville.

"I remember we had an organization meeting where all the minor league managers were supposed to report on their players. Earl Weaver, who was then managing the Oriole's Rochester team in the International League, said that last season he saw the best pitcher he ever saw in all his years in baseball. He wasn't talking about one of our players, he was talking about Tom Seaver, who was then playing for Lynchburg.

"After the meeting, Harry Dalton, our scouting director, came over to me and said, 'Al, you were right about Seaver and we were wrong.' It's nice to get that kind of recognition.

"I gotta go," Al said, "but let me tell you about drugs and baseball. There used to be guys who came around talking how good drugs made them feel. And some of the guys who should have known better listened to them. Willie Mays Aikens was a shy, insecure kid who stuttered. He couldn't wait to feel better and tried drugs. He got hooked and in 1983 during the off-season he was busted and went to jail for a few months. The Royals got rid of him, and he was out of the majors three years later at the age of 31." In 1986, Aikens showed that he could still hit and led the Mexican League with an amazing .454 BA with 154 RBIs. But by then there were no major league takers. Nobody wants to buy trouble. And indeed, on December 13, 1994, Aikens was sentenced to twenty years in jail for drug trafficking.

"I got lots more stories," said Kubski, "But I gotta go and check on some kid prospects. Call me, I'm usually home in the mornings. After that, I'm out working." He was off, this seventy-year-old man who was cutting down on his activities.

LENNY MERULLO

THE NAUGHTY FORTIES

Lenny Merullo is a scout for the Major League Scouting Bureau. He is seventy-five years old with a spirit that only a happily fulfilled man could possess. When you ask him a question, you better write it down. By the time he finishes telling you his wonderful stories, you will have forgotten what you asked him in the first place. But it's well worth the trip. Ask him about the difference between the players of today and those of the 1940s, and Lenny is off and running.

Along the way you will learn that old baseball men are proud of their accomplishments, even the off-beat ones. Until Lenny mentioned it, I wasn't aware that he is still the holder of a forty-three-year-old record that has withstood challenges from tens of thousands of big league games. It's a record not many people make an effort to approach. "I hold the record for the most errors by a shortstop in one inning—4. I made them in a game against the Boston Braves on September 13, 1952, the day my son was born. That's why they nicknamed him 'Boots.' I guess my mind wasn't really on the game that day." Lenny is happy to still be in the record book after all these years. And why not? How many of us can be sure of even this much immortality? As for his positive accomplishments as a Cub player, Lenny takes credit for bringing a truly fine Cincinnati Reds pitcher, Paul Derringer (223 wins, 212 losses; 3.46 ERA) to the Cubs.

Late in the 1942 season Lenny hit a grand slam off Derringer. In the off-season the Reds sold Derringer to the Cubs. "They figured if Merullo could hit a grand slammer off of him, he must be washed up," Lenny said, "But they were wrong. He gave us some good years." Derringer actually helped the Cubs win the pennant in 1945. Naturally, they didn't win the World Series, and they haven't been in a Series since.

Lenny's recollections of how he went into organized ball illustrate the difference between how baseball was looked upon in the 1940s and how it is considered today. Lenny was one of twelve children, a son of parents who had come from Italy. In the '30s, the child of an immigrant who played baseball was an enigma to his parents. He should be out working instead of engaging in a foolish, time-wasting activity. But first-generation American youngsters loved the game for a number of reasons, not the least being that baseball is a complex game not easily understood. Its very arcane nature gave the immigrant child a facility in an activity his parents would never master. Knowing and playing baseball made the child different from his old-country parents. How did the immigrant kid learn baseball? He just absorbed it . Another attraction of baseball was that it served as a rite of passage for the immigrant's son. By playing baseball he became a real American.

Lenny was a standout on his high school team. He was only fifteen years old and already a senior. "It wasn't that I was so smart. It was that the school wanted to graduate kids as early as possible so they could go out and start working full time and help their families. So they kept promoting me." Lenny tried to outfox them and started to lag behind in his studies. He soon was called to the principal's office. The principal was wise to Lenny's ruse. "We know that you want to stay back so you can play another year of baseball," the principal admonished him. "But we're not going to let you do it. You're going to graduate, whether you like it or not." Forced out of the nest, Lenny went to prep school and then to Villanova on a college baseball scholarship.

Lenny had been scouted by the Cubs when he was still in high school and during the summers when he played in sandlot games around the Boston area. They felt that he had great potential, and they brought him out to Wrigley Field in Chicago so the team brass could look him over. They were impressed, and he met P. K. Wrigley, the owner of the Cubs, whom Lenny still refers to as "Mr. Wrigley" with a deference that borders on awe. Wrigley said that the Cubs wanted to sign him, but he would advise that the teenager stay in college and get his degree. The Cubs would be interested in him when he graduated. Then P.K. did something that could have landed the chewing-gum panjandrum in boiling hot water. He handed Lenny fifteen hundred dollars so he would remember the Cubs.

If this arrangement had become known, Lenny's college baseball career would have ended. He would have been declared ineligible and his athletic scholarship withdrawn. Since the Merullo family couldn't afford the tuition at Villanova, Lenny's academic career would also have ended. The Cubs weren't about to say anything about the cozy little arrangement and neither was Lenny. "This was done a lot in those days," Lenny says. "Lou Boudreau, the great Indians short-stop and Hall of Famer, got money from Cleveland that paid his tuition while he played at the University of Illinois. Hank Borowy, a terrific pitcher in the forties, got money from the Yankees while playing for Fordham."

But Lenny's exceptional playing at Villanova caught the eye of Yankee scout Paul Kritchel, who tried to make the same deal with Merullo as he had with Hank Borowy. Lenny told Kritchel, that he was already obligated to the Cubs, and when the Villanova coach, Doc Jacobs found out, he had Merullo declared ineligible.

When P.K. found out about Lenny's dilemma, he gave Merullo $4,000 to finish his college education and invited him to the Cubs' spring training site at Catalina, California. They don't make owners like that anymore. Hell, they don't even make chewing gum like that anymore. Lenny actually got his degree from Boston College by going during the off-season.

As a Cubs scout before he joined the Major League Scouting Bureau, Lenny covered the Northeast. "Before the draft, the Yankees could sign everybody be-cause they had the money and the tradition," Lenny said. But this was a two-edged sword that Merullo used to his advantage. "I would ask a prospect if he'd rather be in the Yankee organization and try to break into the majors with guys like DiMaggio in the Yankee lineup and a farm system that was packed with talent. Or would he rather sign with the Cubs and have a real shot at someday making the club." He sold a lot of kids with that argument.

"I don't want to take credit for the guys who made it big," Merullo said when asked about the "name players" he signed, "because I have a longer list of guys who never made it. If I talk about one, I have to talk about the other." When pressed Lenny mentions with satisfaction that in the late '50s he saw a kid in the Hearst Games Tournament named Ron Santo. He wasn't much of a catcher, but Lenny saw his potential. "We signed him for $18,000," Lenny boasts. Santo was the regular third baseman with the Cubs for fifteen years. As if to show the other side of the ledger, Lenny tells of an outfield prospect named Danny Murphy who was widely sought after in 1960. Merullo was very high on the kid and he talked "Mr. Wrigley" into giving the youngster a $100,000 bonus for signing with the Cubs. Murphy never stuck in the majors. He was up and down for a few years and later had a brief career as a pitcher with the White Sox.

The player whose signing gave Merullo the most satisfaction was Moe Drabowsky. "He was undecided whether to sign with the Cubs or with the White Sox. I met him at the airport. Moe was very intelligent. He later had the reputa-tion of being a practical joker, but he's smart. Anyway, when he came to Chi-cago, he had brought his parents and his sixteen-year-old sister with him, and I took them to Wrigley Field, the long way. I had heard he was considering the White Sox and I wanted to show him the section of town where the old Comiskey Park was in. It was an ugly, old, industrial, run-down area. The Drabowskys didn't say anything, but I could see that they were upset by the landscape. Then

I took the beautiful drive to Wrigley Field which sits in a lovely part of town. He signed with the Cubs." Drabowsky had a fine seventeen year career as a reliever in the majors.

Unlike a number of other veteran scouts, Lenny is very high on the role of the Major League Scouting Bureau. "It's not because I work for them, but they do a great service for the clubs. We bird-dog talent that the clubs might have overlooked. And it's a big savings for them when we do the scouting. We've come up with a lot of the top players in the game today." Lenny, however, feels as most of the other veteran scouts when he discusses the younger scouts: He doesn't hold them in high regard. Merullo refers to them as "computer scouts" who rely solely on numbers because they lack the experience and baseball instincts that the older scouts have developed in their long years in the game. Lenny warms to the subject: "They think they're more important than the ballplayer. When you try to sign a prospect, you still have to make his parents comfortable. It may be the first time the kid's been away from home. Now, a young scout may be only ten years older than the kid he's trying to sign. If you're a parent, are you going to trust your kid to another kid?"

Merullo has a deep appreciation and affection for his fellow veteran scouts. "You ought to talk to Howie Haak. He's got a lot of great stories," Lenny said, as if he doesn't. Told that he doesn't sound anywhere near his age, Lenny says what practically every older scout said, "Baseball keeps you young."

The young septuagenarian is the founder of a modest Merullo dynasty. His son "Boots" played in the minors for three seasons, and his grandson Matt was drafted by the White Sox in 1986 and led the American Association with a .332 batting average at Nashville in 1993. If you want to talk baseball, you want to talk to Lenny Merullo.

STEVE SOUCHOCK

ON THE TRAIL

The owner of the Cincinnati Reds and the doyenne of dysfunctional thinking, Marge Schott, once asked in her insensitive way, "Why do we pay these guys [scouts] just for sitting and watching ball games?" If you're a scout and you haven't already despaired of teaching Schott anything, you might want to tell her what you do and how guys like you provide the fuel to keep her money-making machine running. Or as Tiger scout Steve Souchock put it, with the generosity of an elder statesman, "She should take three days off and travel with a scout, and I think she would better understand how scouts work." He didn't say whether the Schott dogs would ride in front or in back.

Steve Souchock is a seventy-five-year-old scout with the Detroit Tigers. When he was a player he was a good utility man, starting with the Yankees in 1946. But with an outfield of DiMaggio, Henrich, and Keller, Steve couldn't break into the regular lineup. In 1948 the Yankee outfield of DiMaggio, Henrich, and Lindell had a combined batting average of .312. After the season Steve was traded to the White Sox and wound up his playing days at Detroit in 1955. He's been a scout for over thirty-five years.

Steve's attitude about how scouts are appreciated is "They tell scouts they are the backbone of baseball, yet they don't pay them enough, and they're also the first to get fired." Many of the older scouts receive only enough to supplement their Social Security and bring them up to the allowable maximum. In effect, the club owners look to the American public to subsidize their veteran scouts. There are megamillions available for stars who may or may not produce for a team, but when it comes to economizing, most organizations start with the scouts and office workers.

Steve has seen and signed some of the best in baseball, and he's accomplished this by dedication and a seeming imperviousness to the rigors of the road. As he says, "One thing about a scout. He learns how to read a map. It's amazing how many people want to become scouts. I know a judge who really loves the game and wants to scout. But there is a lot more to it than just sitting at games."

Let's imagine what a day is like for a major league scout like Steve. Let's say he's covering Southern California, which is a great deal of geography to begin with. It's like covering Great Britain, except the tea is worse. Let's say that there's a high school kid in Bakersfield who's knocking 'em dead. So off you go in your car to see this kid. The game starts after school, somewhere around 3:00 P.M. Have you ever gone to Bakersfield on an afternoon in June? Don't.

You try to find a tree to park under because having your car bombarded by the resident birds is better than searing your hand later when you try to open the car door that's been baking in the desert sun for hours. You check to see if you're in the right place, introduce yourself to the coaches, and take a seat. Take any seat. There are plenty of them because no one watches a high school baseball game unless he's an unemployed relative of one of the players or he's been sentenced to do this as part of his community service. So you sit there in the sun. Some sun worshipers might think this is a good chance to get a nice tan; it's actually a good chance to be get burned to a cinder. There is no shade because high school fields are just that—fields. You sit on a splintery plank and try to accustom your eyes to the glare that rivals that of an atomic bomb test.

Finally the game starts. Now, if the kid you're watching is a fielder, you get a chance to see him do his thing—unless. Unless he has paid more attention to his batting than his algebra and has been declared ineligible. The principal doesn't call you with the news. It's hard enough breaking it to the coach. In a case like this you try and salvage something by chatting with the coaches of the two teams. You give them your card and ask them to let you know in the future if they see a real good prospect. If they do, you'll send someone from the organization that you're not too fond of. And since the human body was not constructed with high school baseball in mind, you exit as soon as you can.

Let's suppose that your luck had not run out somewhere north of Barstow. The kid you want to look at is playing. If he has a good day, you feel you haven't wasted your time. You take notes and later in the motel you will write up your report. However, is the kid really this good or is he having an extraordinarily good day? We all have them. The day when everything falls into place and you're better than you really are. So you must be careful about your evaluation based on this one big day. How fast is he getting down the line; on the bases? How about his bat speed? Does he have good rhythm at the plate or is there a hitch or loop in his swing? And if so, can it be corrected or should it be? How does he field his position? What kind of an arm does he have? If he's an out-fielder, how much ground can he cover? If he's an infielder, how well does he go to his right? To his left?

The situation with judging a pitcher is different. But it can be a good news/bad news situation. If the kid is on the mound long enough, you get a good look at him. Fifty or sixty pitches tells a scout a lot about a prospect. How are his basics? How fast is his fastball? Does he have a curve? A changeup? A slider? How is his pickoff move? Does he have any bad habits that must be addressed such as throwing across his body?

Problems arise when the pitching prospect you're watching has an off day. You can tell a lot by how he handles the basics of pitching, yet a kid who gets knocked around in a high school game doesn't inspire a scout with confidence. The trouble is that you're not about to stick around until the kid gets another turn. You'd rather die, and that's a real possibility during relentless desert days. Or perhaps your prospect is also a good hitter, as Dwight Gooden or Brett Saberhagen were in high school. And perhaps the coach, whose job is to win games, has played the kid in the field when he wasn't pitching. On the day you see him, the kid might have been a regular in three or four games before his turn to pitch. If his arm is tired—and whose wouldn't be—he won't look too good and you're left guessing about him.

The abiding concern about any high school prospect is what kind of kid he seems like. Could there be problems down the road when he is away from home, on his own at seventeen or eighteen years of age. Do you think he's the kind of kid who will be able to cope with the temptations that will challenge his limited experience? You put down your informed guess in your report and hope for the best.

Okay, let's say that you're having one of your good days. You see the kid, he's impressed you, and now you're free to get some shade. Your face feels like a Big Mac just before they put on the special sauce. You go back to your motel, which is as modest as you can find, and hope that the centipedes, scorpions, and other desert fauna haven't set up house in your room. Since your per diem is calculated at just below survival level, you search out the local Arby's or other fast-food emporiums where gourmet cooking means that they toast the bun.

Early the next morning it starts all over, and you're once again on your way to some other town that you hope is on the map. And you do this for at least 150 days out of the year. Sometimes you get home after two weeks, but you don't count on it. Your wife never seems to get used to your erratic schedule and tries to help you figure out a more sensible routine that will bring you home for weekends. It doesn't ever seem to work the way she wants it to.

You're a one-man operation, so you throw the bags into the trunk and you battle the elements and leads that go sour, and you try to stare down bad luck. Somehow you manage to do all that. But there's one battle you never seem to win. The battle against loneliness.

Hey Marge Schott, ever been really lonely? Think about it some night in that large, empty house of yours. And then maybe, just maybe you might realize that you have something in common with those guys you pay just to sit and watch ballgames.

Here's a story that Steve Souchock swears is true:

"A few years ago there was a scout who went up the central part of the state to see a young player in high school. The school was outside of town, and the player was getting a lot of attention. The scout got lost and drove into a small airport to ask about the location of the ballfield. They told him they have helicopters to take people on tours, etc., and said that they could find the ballfield for a price. The scout said, 'Let's go,' and the pilot found the park in a few minutes and asked the scout if he wanted him to land. The scout, afraid that he would never find the place again if he drove, told him to put the copter down and that he'd get a ride back somehow after the game. The pilot, a hot dog, put the copter down in the middle of center field. The scout got out. That day there were a lot of other scouts at the game and they gave him a standing ovation. This may have been the first time a scout ever used a helicopter. But it so happened that the scout's boss was also at the game to check on the prospect and told the scout that he was even more curious to see how the scout was going to put this trip on his expense account."

INDEX